Career Compass

Titles in the Series

The U.S. Naval Institute
Blue & Gold Professional Library

For more than one hundred years, U.S. Navy professionals have counted on specialized books published by the Naval Institute Press to prepare them for their responsibilities as they advance in their careers and to serve as ready references and refreshers when needed. From the days of coal-fired battleships to the era of unmanned aerial vehicles and laser weaponry, such perennials as *The Bluejacket's Manual* and the *Watch Officer's Guide* have guided generations of Sailors through the complex challenges of naval service. As these books are updated and new ones are added to the list, they will carry the distinctive mark of the Blue & Gold Professional Library series to remind and reassure their users that they have been prepared by naval professionals and they meet the exacting standards that Sailors have long expected from the U.S. Naval Institute.

Career Compass

**Navigating through the Navy's Officer
Assignment and Promotion Systems**

James A. Winnefeld Sr.

Naval Institute Press
Annapolis, Maryland

Naval Institute Press
291 Wood Road
Annapolis, MD 21402

Excerpts from *Bugles and a Tiger: A Personal Adventure* by John Masters originally
appeared in *The Atlantic Monthly*
Copyright 1956 by John Masters
Copyright renewed 1984 by Barbara Masters
Reprinted by permission of Brandt & Hochman Literary Agents, Inc.

Library of Congress Cataloging-in-Publication Data
Winnefeld, James A., 1929–
    Career compass : navigating through the Navy's officer assignment and pro-
motion systems / James A. Winnefeld, Sr.
        p. cm. — (U.S. Naval Institute blue & gold professional library)
    Includes bibliographical references and index.
    ISBN 1-59114-963-0 (alk. paper)
    1. United States. Navy—Promotions. 2. United States. Navy—Officers' hand-
books. I. Title. II. Series.
VB313.W55 2005
359.'0023'73—dc22

                                                                        2004026835

Printed in the United States of America on acid-free paper ∞
12 11 10 09 08 07 06 05   9 8 7 6 5 4 3 2
First printing

This book is dedicated to two former superintendents of the United States Naval Academy and three Naval Academy classes:

To Vice Adm. William Mack, a gentleman and naval officer of the old school, who was my author-mentor and friend and who demonstrated daily what love of the service is all about.

And to Adm. Kinnaird McKee, friend, classmate, role model, and the embodiment of the finest ideals of the naval service.

And to the Naval Academy classes of 1951, 1980, and 1981. I started my naval career with my classmates of 1951 and along the way swore in the midshipmen of the classes of 1980 and 1981. Good shipmates all, and a Sailor can ask for no more.

Performance: The execution of an action; something accomplished; deed, feat.

—*Webster's Seventh New Collegiate Dictionary*

We may give you advice, but we cannot inspire conduct.

—Duc François de La Rochefoucauld, *Maxims,* 1665

Contents

Foreword

I can still vividly recall my father, a retired USMC colonel, giving me his sole piece of advice on my career as I set out from the Naval Academy in the late 1970s: "Always remember, Jim, that your detailer is just as interested in your career and professional development as you are in his." A somewhat cynical view, and with all respect to my wonderful dad, I think I would have benefited far more from Rear Adm. Jim Winnefeld's outstanding compendium of career advice. This book should be in the hands of every newly commissioned officer, and it clearly would benefit many of our senior folks to pick up a copy as well. You are about to embark on an extremely entertaining and informative journey as you read it.

Laying out a well-charted and extremely thoughtful course, Admiral Winnefeld has drawn on his own experiences during three tours in the bureau, as well as on the collected wisdom of many others. The sources who have contributed reflect not only experienced officers on active duty today—there is, for example, a wonderful appendix by a detailer—but also those with the deeper perspective afforded by retirement. The book is full of simple but powerful insights that run the gamut from explaining what really goes into the mythic "service reputation" to how our spouses are involved in our careers in today's modern world, from what truly matters in terms of flag selection to the pros and cons of graduate education. I can easily think of a half-dozen times during my own career where access to a commonsense volume like this would have been extraordinarily helpful.

Best of all is the clear, clean philosophy Admiral Winnefeld lays out. This is no "careerist handbook." The approach the admiral takes is all about service, dignity, and love of country. This is a book written for all the right reasons, and I would with pride unhesitatingly give this to an officer from another service and say, "Here is the Navy's balanced approach to a career, described by someone who has sailed at sea and served ashore in the toughest jobs." As Admiral Winnefeld says again and again, there are no silver bullets, no gimmicks, no slick path to success—it is all about performance at sea and ashore, in that order. This book gets it all just right in terms of tone and integrity.

There is also a plethora of practical advice herein that will help a young officer hit the right balance between high energy "can-do" enthusiasm and coming on a little too strong—so that their boss needs to provide "fire control, not fire power." Full of great anecdotes and personal experiences, what this book does best is help a good officer capitalize on his or her strengths while avoiding many common career pitfalls. The advice in this volume will keep any officer sailing smoothly in the middle of the channel. As you read through it and map your own career against the advice within these pages, you will find a well-laid course indeed.

Vice Adm. James G. Stavridis, USN

Preface

This book is a user's manual to help naval officers understand the key role of performance in assignments and promotions. It is intended to remove some of the mystery surrounding the process of rising in a naval career. The target audience is naval officers across the seniority ladder but particularly junior officers. The latter are encouraged to look on this book as a complement to the existing excellent guides on watch standing and the duties of a division officer. Although intended principally for the junior officer, it also covers the later stages of a naval career. This broader coverage has two purposes: to reach a larger audience and to inform the junior officer of what lies down the road. Hence, the book's coverage is broad but is in less depth when the discussion turns to performance in command, promotion to senior rank, and ultimately retirement. Junior readers will benefit from seeing the forest as well as the trees.

A certain amount of skepticism is in order when one sets oneself up to convey enduring lessons of conduct and advice on career advancement. This healthy skepticism benefits both the author and the reader in considering the "obvious." Dr. Samuel Johnson once remarked, "It is sometimes necessary to belabor the obvious because it is so often overlooked." There is much that is obvious in this book: for example, the strong emphasis on professional performance in your current billet and in preparing yourself to relieve your seniors if the need arises.

Moreover, there is little that is original in this book. The text draws without apology from many experts and astute observers of the Navy's system for advancing its best officers. Many of the book's sources have skillfully navigated through the shoals and rocks of long careers and emerged at or near the top of their profession. Luck is part of it, but even more to the point is great skill in understanding what the business is about and devising ways to ensure it prospers. The book is not intended as a critique of the system, or as a hymn of praise. Rather, the objective is to explain the system in simple terms and cast the narrative in such a way as to lead the serving officer through channels that are not always well defined and to point out adverse currents, obstacles, and dead ends as well as significant navigation marks.

Although the words "promotion" and "assignment" are in the subtitle of the book, those words are intended to tempt the reader. The book is really about performance—demonstrated professional capability. *Performance is the sine qua non of promotion.* To sermonize about performance, however, is to emphasize the labor-intensive part of the system and risk losing the audience. To discuss the promotion and assignment systems is to dangle a carrot in front of the reader. Therefore, this book discusses performance, assignment, and promotion as a unit because they are inextricably intertwined.

Current procedures, practices, and instructions are referenced occasionally in the text to provide a rough, current, and relevant baseline. If experience is any guide, however, all will change over time. To avoid making the book unnecessarily time bound, I have furnished some historical perspective and emphasized basic principles. There is a risk to this more contextual approach: some of the details of the evolving "current" system may be in error. In order not to discredit the whole on the basis of an old snapshot, I am asking readers to look for the shape of the forest and the terrain rather than focus on a few familiar trees in their path—or, to use the nautical metaphor, focus on the channel rather than on a single navigational mark that may be misplaced.

Before we begin this journey through the Navy's system of officer performance and advancement, the reader might well ask: why is this book not written by an active duty officer, preferably one currently assigned to the Naval Personnel Command, who is up to date on every detail of the current systems and is still in the race? The following response is offered. Retired officers have the experience and a longer perspective of how the system has evolved and continues to change. They are in a better position to see what is enduring and what may be the fad of the moment. Being at some remove from the current system, but nevertheless familiar with it, they can examine the whole critically, with charity and with some detachment. They are in a better position to "tell it like it is," or was, without fear of offending those who have had a major role in the shape of the current officer advancement environment.

With these preliminaries behind us, let us examine the Navy ethos and practice as it relates to officer performance, assignment, and advancement, starting with the sine qua non of performance.

Acknowledgments

Many excellent officers, reviewers, and editors have made this book better than would have been the case had I "steamed independently." I owe a particular debt of gratitude to Vice Adm. Robert F. Dunn, USN (Ret.) and Comdr. Clay Harris USN, then commanding officer of the USS *Arleigh Burke,* for reviewing the first draft of the book and keeping me in the channel. I also benefited from a review of a later draft by Vice Adm. James F. Calvert, USN (Ret.). Most of their suggestions have been incorporated herein. I also wish to extend my thanks to Mr. Dwight Stanton of the Naval Personnel Command (NPC), who arranged for a review of chapters 18 and 19 by the NPC staff. These early reviewers are not responsible for errors and opinions expressed in the text.

I owe much to Mr. Tom Cutler, senior acquisitions editor of the Naval Institute Press, for his encouragement and for piloting my first draft through the press's review process. My thanks also go to Ms. Jennifer Till for her help in compiling and selecting the photographs in the book. Ms. Linda W. O'Doughda, managing editor of the press, and Ms. Patti Bower were the key persons in shepherding the book through the production process. Finally, my deep gratitude goes to Ms. Kathy Swain, the copy editor of the book, who gave me an excellent refresher course in English usage and did so with humor and understanding.

Career Compass

1

Performance

The Sine Qua Non

The quality of your naval career, whether short or long, is solely dependent on your performance. Whether you get the plum assignments and whether or not you get promoted is based solely and wholly on your performance.

—Vice Adm. Robert F. Dunn, USN (Ret.)

The simple truth is that promotions are granted for superior past performance, the potential for future superior performance, and the needs of the service for your skills. There is no short cut, fast track, or glory road to the ultimate prize of professional development. You cannot buy it whatever your wealth, connections, and skill in manipulation. One of the glories of the naval service is that it comes down to *you*, what *you* put into the quest and your acquired inventory of professional skills.

Luck can, and sometimes does, play a role. But one cannot and should not look to luck to overcome insufficient diligence and preparation. To excuse one's own assignment and promotion disappointments as "bad luck" and to explain a colleague's success as "good luck" is one explanation of the speaker's shortcomings.

Naval promotions are not a lottery in which only the lucky win and only the unlucky lose. Everyone at some point fails of selection. Even the Chief of Naval Operations (CNO) or other four-star officer can fail of selection for a follow-on assignment. All officers, whether active, retired, or reserve, have a favorite "what if" story in their own career history. They were not screened or selected for some job or rank, or they experienced some other career disappointment. These comments often are, and are seen as, excuses. I will discuss career disappointments and their handmaiden excuses more in a later chapter.

The beginning of wisdom, and indeed the focal point of much of our precommissioning (precom) education, is to take responsibility for our own actions or our failure to take action. We cannot avoid this responsibility, and if our words or actions are to the contrary, we have faulted on the major premise of our commission.

Before returning to performance as the theme of this chapter and indeed the book as a whole, I need to say a word about that misunderstood and much-maligned term "the ambitious officer." Marcus Aurelius wrote that "a man's worth is no greater than his ambitions," but in our culture there is considerable ambivalence about the word "ambitious." Although we value success, we seem also to want our leaders to be without personal ambition. But most successful naval leaders would not want in their commands an officer without ambition and the will to succeed. Ambition is the engine that drives the service, ambition based on solid performance and oriented to the unit's mission.

Ambition has received a bad reputation because it is often confused with self-serving, grasping, and unscrupulous habits. Ambition overdone—just as is any good quality that is overdone—is dangerous to the person and his or her environment. The properly ambitious officer tempers zeal with a concern for others, particularly subordinates, and with a sense of mission that is not intended to benefit any individual. *Ambition properly exercised is focused on the mission, not on the career enhancement and promotion of the individual.* Although this book seems at first glance to be about the promotion system and ambition, it is really about the service's mission and the *performance* of its component parts.

Most successful naval officers are not noted for their introspection. But all, either knowingly or not, keep themselves and their tasks in perspective.

They do want to be promoted, but first of all they want to do a tough job well and only second seek the regard of fellow officers and the crew. The old nautical adage of "ship, shipmate, self" is still good advice. The most dangerous naval officers, and there are a few in any organization, are those who want to be promoted at any price. When they game the system, they do it to achieve personal advantage. These officers see life as a zero-sum game, gloat about the professional misfortunes of others, are loath to share the credit for a job well done, look at every challenge with an eye to what is in it for them, and look for their next job before they really settle into their current one. They are not officers; they are careerists. And the demands of the profession uncover them sooner or later. Striking a balance between ambition and service is among the most crucial judgments officers make as they proceed through a naval career.

Good Performance as the Independent Variable

Good performance in your current job is the entering argument in qualifying for promotion. But good performance in a lesser job is not as persuasive as good performance in a tough job. Even better is good performance in a tough job under tough conditions. Best of all is a combination of the above with the result being recorded by an able writer of reports of fitness. Note how performance enters into each step of this process:

1. Qualifying for a demanding job in the first place
2. Performing well in a tough job
3. Performing while forward deployed, in combat, or both
4. Serving under a skipper who can document performance in a way that is convincing to a selection or screening board.

Although luck plays some role in each step of the process, ambitious officers exert themselves at each step, luck or not. For example, qualifying for a demanding job means seeking logical precursor assignments, working on the deck plates to become a professional, and looking for and not avoiding the tough jobs. Some officers try to avoid the arduous and sometimes thankless jobs in the mistaken belief that all division officer or department head jobs are the same. Why not prepare for or pick the one that has the least risk or work associated with it? Why not pick the one where the challenges are those with which one is most comfortable? Don't do it! You will only set yourself up for disappointment.

Those who perform the toughest jobs under the most demanding conditions are the career winners. Some opt for the most congenial homeport and operations schedule rather than assignments that test their mettle. Others try to snivel out of a deployment or to cut it short with clever manipulation. But the real pros want to be tested and found up to snuff—just as a good football team wants to go up against champions rather than patsies. Do you have a nose for the ball or for the sideline and the water bucket?

Then keep in mind that even when it comes to writing your fitness report you are not without influence. Skippers want and are directed to obtain your input before the first draft report is written. They want you to tell them about your accomplishments and your desires as to future assignments. The trick is to give your busy executive officer (XO) and skipper phrases, sentences, and even paragraphs that can be lifted with little change into your fitness report. This is not a sneaky or underhanded endeavor. Skippers and XOs are busy people, as you will find out, and the easier you make their jobs, the more your true value is appreciated and documented. They are human; they cannot remember everything. It is up to you to help them tactfully and without fanfare. A side benefit of this preparation is that you will learn to write reports of fitness before you get in the skipper's chair.

Still, you may encounter at least one difficult assignment environment where you will prepare yourself, work hard, and do all the right things—and may not get all the credit you believe you deserve. Unfortunately, such environments sometimes include duty on a commissioning crew or in a ship in overhaul. Although the best people are picked for the precom crew, such assignments are not under the same spotlight as overseas deployments. The better assignments for making a mark involve overseas deployments, not taking a ship through overhaul. Not only is a ship to be commissioned or in overhaul not operational, but also to some degree your future is hostage to the shipyard's vagaries, workload, and schedule. Nevertheless, if you get such an assignment you cannot let down. You must do your absolute best, and, if you do, you can rest assured your reputation will be enhanced. Some officers have made their service reputation—and eventually flag rank—by being assigned to a ship in a yard and in trouble. Their task was to get the ship out of the yard and ready for deployment. Overcoming past shortcomings of management or leadership gave them a great stage on which to perform.

Needs of the Service

The handmaiden of good professional performance is that oft-misused phrase "needs of the service." What does it mean? In short, it means billets that need to be filled, the priority accorded to filling them, and the quality of the officer needed to fill them. "Quality" means the qualifications of the officer needed (experience and education). Quality involves a performance dimension as well as the credentials dimension. For example, some billets call for a postcommand commander who, at a minimum, had a command tour that was successful.

The phrase "needs of the service" is often used to justify assignment to a billet the officer so assigned does not want. It could be a good billet—command—and the officer assigned has just come from a successful command tour. Sometimes an officer who had just returned home from a command tour in a deployed unit was "ripped out" and sent to another similar command (perhaps deployed) where the previous skipper had been hospitalized or relieved for other reasons. The needs of the service dictated a quick transfer at considerable personal cost to the officer so moved. At least one officer during his career commanded three aircraft carriers—in part because of a similar daisy chain. He did well in all three and was a shoe-in for flag rank.

But more often, the needs of the service send you to an assignment that is difficult to fill for another reason. No one wants it, or it has been left vacant ("gapped") too long. Your negotiating power is limited in these circumstances, but you might either negotiate a deal with the detailer to short tour you in such a job or perform so well that you warrant special treatment for a follow-on assignment. To find yourself in such an unwanted job will try your soul. It has happened at least once in many careers, and the only way the officer could overcome the handicap was to redouble efforts to achieve top performance—to the point where the detailer could not afford to leave the officer there. Detailers have a demand for more top-quality officers than exist. So they must husband or direct this quality resource carefully. One cannot afford to put top officers into less-demanding or low-leverage jobs.

But there is another dimension to needs of the service. Some sub-specialties will be in more demand today than they were yesterday. Some trends can be predicted, and others cannot. You should attempt to acquire professional tools that will be most needed in the Navy of the future. Every so often officers will be promoted, even to high rank, not because they were at the top in the performance dimension but because they had a specialty that was critically needed at their selected rank. So although performance is the most important horse in the race, credentials can become a critical factor in some cases.

Although it is a truism to state that we carry the seeds of future promotions in our performance to date, this obvious fact is often obscured by our obsession with the politics of the game—and luck, both good and bad. There is simply no easy path to command and promotions. You must get the selection board's trust the old-fashioned way: you must earn it. It is not a matter of touching all the bases in a good career progression. You must be a solid hitter, one who hits the ball in the clutch and hits solidly and well not over just an inning or a game but for the entire season of a career. It is not the warfare pins you wear, the decorations on your chest, or the people you know; it is how you do the job that counts. It helps if the job is tough, the environment is tougher, and your skipper is toughest. But it starts and ends with you.

2

Your Boss Wants to See You Promoted but Needs Your Help

If you and your boss don't get along, it is not the boss's fault.

—Anonymous

A little remembered fact is that your boss benefits when you are promoted. You are or become one of that individual's "team." No matter how cantankerous the person is, no matter how off-putting, no matter how demanding, your skipper wants to see you succeed. One can argue: on their terms or mine? But they are your bosses. All skippers glory in a high retention rate and a high promotion rate in their command. After all, it is a testimonial to their leadership that you "shipped over" or were promoted. Most will be bashful about it, but they attribute your correct thinking and promotion to their training, nurturing, and cuffing when needed. No skipper ever took joy in a low shipping-over rate or promotion rate. The point is that you have a built-in advantage as you strive to perform well in your current billet: your skipper wants you to succeed, and most will work hard to see that you do. But your skipper cannot do it alone.

Be skeptical when you hear the comment, "My skipper had it in for me." When you pull the string on that comment, you often hear such self-serving excuses as "Well, I didn't kowtow to him," "I told her like it was," "I stood up for my people," "I didn't make him look good," "I didn't brown nose her," and so on. You get the idea. Behind each excuse lies the real reason, which is less flattering to the speaker. Your skipper deserves your study, not your excuses. You study your skippers not only because your future success is in their hands but also because you just might learn from them. Skippers are human, but they also have a job to do. That job is rarely easy, and skippers must do their job through the efforts of you and your shipmates. If they cannot do that, they fail.

As you mature in the service, you come to realize that the real heavy lifting of the Navy's work does not get done through peremptory orders (though some are needed) but through guiding and motivating subordinates. If you seem to be getting an inordinate amount of undesired, and in your perception undeserved, attention from your skipper, it is probably the result of the judgment that you need prodding, guidance, or butt kicking to get the command's and your jobs done. You can fight your skippers on this, or you can learn from them. The former may make you feel better and more self-righteous (momentarily), but the latter is the more constructive course. Everyone has had some bosses one did not like, but there is not a single one from whom the subordinate could not learn and become a better officer for it. The point of all this: make your skipper your ally in the performance and promotion business, not your adversary. How is this done? Let us look at a few paths you might explore.

Who Is the "Go-to" Officer in Your Outfit?

Every command has a small number of more junior officers who are so versatile, so willing to do the toughest jobs, so full of gusto and a sense of adventure that they become in effect the 911 staff for the command. Special or priority projects migrate to them—not because they need to be dumped on but because they are so able, willing, and can do. They are the treasures of the command, the first people the commanding officer (CO), XO, or department head turn to when they need something important done in a hurry and done well. Most often the task falls outside the younger officer's narrow billet description. No matter, though; they get on with it, and a miracle occurs: they get their shipmates to help them or smooth the path for them.

You may follow the old salt's advice and never volunteer and never offer unsolicited information, but you can also never try to get out of an onerous task. Your reputation will spread like wildfire where it counts. It is not that you are a pushover, it is that you are a person to give the really tough and often dirty jobs to. A reputation like that is twenty-four carat at fitness report time. Having read thousands of fitness reports while serving on various boards, I can confirm that the "can-do" folks bore through to the minds of the board members.

Who Is the Most Positive Officer in Your Outfit?

Every command has its share of gloomy gusses, skeptics, and sour apples. They never met an order or a boss they liked. They are the first to see the difficulties, shortcomings, loopholes, and downside of any order or task they are given. Their long-term objective is get to their active duty release date (RAD) or rotation date, and their short-term objective seems to be to make life as depressing as possible for their shipmates. As a result they are hard to get moving, and they question the need for the task and the way it is to be done. They are never morale boosters, and their best company is like-minded souls.

On the other hand there are the enthusiasts, the "red hots," "let's get it done yesterday" types who are the outfit's hard chargers. They occasionally overrun or miss the mark but never have to be prodded. It is their boss's job to provide fire control, not firepower. Although no wardroom or ready room needs many of these people, they really stand out and are the joy of most skippers. Those skippers will forgive them a lot so long as they are responsible and willing to be instructed. Enthusiasm is catching. It may not be stylish to some, but it is guaranteed to get your skipper's attention, and you will soon find the tough and good jobs coming your way.

Do You Have the Solution to the Problem?

For some people it is sufficient to frame the problem. Therein lies the distinction between analysts and executives. Executives must not only correctly formulate the problem but also solve it. Never, ever take a problem to the boss without (at least in your own mind) also developing a range of solutions. And you do not have a lot of time. You cannot take the time to do a study of the options and the costs and benefits. You must be ready now, and this takes some mental preparation before the problem is encountered.

Find out what the command's problems are and practice in your mind what the various solutions might be and what you would do about them if you were in command. I call this "mentally fleeting up." It should be part of your daily training. Start thinking in terms of "if I were in the skipper's shoes." This training can start at the ensign level and be refined as you get more experience.

In addition to this mental preparation, seize every opportunity to train yourself to think on your feet. When a question is posed to someone else, put yourself through the mental gymnastics of formulating your own answer. Mental agility and a nose for the fundamentals in any situation will serve you well at every step in your career. Most times the good fast solution is better than the better tardy one.

When You Are the Briefer, Do You Know the Subject Better Than Anyone Else?

Briefings are one of the keys to your future. Whether it is a briefing to your fellow officers in the wardroom or ready room or a briefing for the CNO, your service reputation either is being built or rests on the outcome. This book is not a primer on public speaking or "briefmanship." Suffice to say that you should get all the practice you can and prepare yourself meticulously for every presentation. Every reasonable question must be anticipated and an answer prepared. Briefers must mentally sit in the chairs of the audience and judge whether they have achieved clarity, completeness, and purpose. Does the briefing lead to a conclusion and a recommendation, or does it lead to another briefing?

Your primary objective in preparing for a briefing is simple: you must know more about the subject than anybody else in the room. You are assumed by your audience to be the expert. If you are not, someone else should be giving the briefing. Your second objective must be to package the information in a form the audience can understand.

A briefing is a test of your ability to organize your thoughts, present material in a logical manner, and communicate visually and orally. It is also a test of your ability to think on your feet, deal with the unexpected, and exercise tact while conveying information. Careers have been made on superlative briefing skills and in-depth knowledge of the subject being briefed. The Navy's Fighter Weapons School (Top Gun) recognizes the importance of these skills and places extraordinary emphasis on them in qualifying both instructors and students. Repetitive "murder boards," which are group critiques of briefing content, format, and delivery, put each neophyte instructor and student-briefer through the wringer. It is time well spent, and students and members of the staff gain a skill that will serve them well throughout their lives.

Is There a Writer in the House?

Whereas good warfare specialty performance is the bedrock of a naval officer's professional competence, good writing skills are arguably second. Many officers have good warfare specialty skills; alas, few have good writing skills. At some point you will observe that the good job or the career-enhancing task seeks out the good writer. In any ship or squadron (or office), usually only a few officers are also good writers, that is, those who can use good English to powerful effect. Clarity, brevity, and directness are the prized characteristics.

Acquiring this skill takes hard work and practice. Put your best effort into anything written that goes up the chain of command. An excellent place to practice is in writing the performance evaluations for your enlisted men and women. This practice will carry over later in your career in writing reports of fitness on your officers. See a problem? Put it in writing. Such writing not only polishes your drafting skills but also teaches the fundamentals of clear thinking. Official reports are your command's stage on which its performance is viewed. If you can write the tough or delicate paper, report, or letter for the skipper, you will be considered a treasure.

Are You a Pro?

Your most important skill is professional competence. Do you "know your stuff"? Do you skate to get by, or are you the person your chief petty officer or department head knows has the right answers or knows where to get them? Professional competence is so fundamental that it overrides such faults as a colorless or abrasive personality, poor writing style, poor manners, a sloppy uniform, or lack of initiative. I am not suggesting these failings are trivial, only that if you are professionally competent you are worth the effort expended to shape you up. This means that if you are the main propulsion assistant (MPA), you know more about the engineering plant than any officer in the ship—including your boss, whose span of control is much larger. If your boss is more informed about your job than you are—and you do not change that relationship over time—that individual is doing your job for you. You know your plant and your division better than the boss does—or else.

To be called a pro by your shipmates and squadron mates is the ultimate accolade. It is the one you must strive hardest to achieve. It lies completely within your power to achieve it. Your skipper will be one of the first to sense your achievement and applaud it.

If there is a single most important building block to a successful career, becoming a pro is it. It is your primary objective from the first day after you report aboard. Being a pro also means you are not looking around the corner at your next job: you are doing the one you have been assigned—and doing it very well.

Do You Help Your Command Solve People Problems?

Most of the problems and challenges faced by a ship or squadron involve people. Every officer in the command has a role in seeing that subordinates are led well, with sensitivity, and with an eye to making each member of the unit a contributor to the command's mission. That role does not change as you rise in rank and take on more responsible positions; your central focus remains the mission and the subordinates you are trying to motivate, direct, and care for.

Unfortunately, some officers create more personnel problems than they solve. Sometimes this is a matter of inexperience, in other cases it is a matter of personal style in interactions, and in still others it is a matter of interpersonal misunderstandings. On the other hand, some officers seem to be personnel problem solvers. They know their subordinates, they maintain open communications up and down, and they deftly use the tools at their disposal. They know what problems they can help solve, and they know when they need the help of their seniors.

This book is not about "deck plates leadership." It is about professional performance that leads to command and promotions, yet interpersonal skills are a critical element in that performance mix. Look closely at your shipmates who lead enlisted personnel well. In most cases you will find that they are good listeners, they empathize with their subordinates' problems, they do not take themselves too seriously, and they are firm in insisting on high standards for themselves and those who work for them. When you have to appear with one of your subordinates at Captain's Mast, you should ask yourself how you and the errant Sailor got there and what you might have done differently. Likewise, when you see the promotion lists, you should ask yourself why more of your people were not on it.

Perhaps the best reputation you can gain within your command is one of fostering *respect* between you and your subordinates, being a person who knows his or her Sailors, and being the officer who instinctively understands the reaction on the mess decks to a change in policy or circumstance. This raises a related point. Do not avoid assignments to departments or divisions that involve leading large numbers of enlisted personnel. Such assignments might be a source of problems over which your control is limited. On the other hand, Sailor-leading duties present opportunities that more than balance out potential problems. You will be a better executive officer and skipper if you understand your Sailors on the basis of having had daily and close contact with them.

This chapter has covered just a few of the skills that will bring your performance to the attention of the skipper. Inevitably these skills will find their way into your fitness reports and thence to the promotion selection boards.

3

What Are They Saying about You?

Your reputation is a priceless asset; guard it zealously. Do not suc-
cumb to any act which has the possibility to destroy in an instant
the respectability you have earned over a lifetime.

—Rafael C. Benitez, *Anchors: Ethical and Practical Maxims*

It is a small world. The Navy is not as big as you may think. Your reputation is making the rounds—and has been for years. It is built like a house,
brick by brick, good tour by good tour. You have a vested interest in seeing that your reputation is a good one. Your reputation is defined by more
than just a solid or subpar professional performance. Are you a good shipmate? Do you take care of your people? Are you overly concerned with
your own promotion or assignments? Is your family an asset or a drag on
your reputation? Do you drink a bit too much? Are you a good friend and
colleague? The composite of all these factors defines your reputation. It
is passed by word of mouth at any gathering of officers or their spouses.
You will hear questions like the following: "Since you just came from USS
Neversail, you must know Ben So-and-so." "While you were going through
Top Gun, was Lieutenant X on the staff?" "Was Commander Blow still
there when you were at the War College?" And on it goes. Although some
of this is gossip, most of it is an attempt to catch up on news of friends
and to establish links among people in conversation.

John Masters, a career army officer and later a successful novelist,
wrote a memoir of his growing up as a junior officer in the Indian army

of the 1930s. He had many bumps in his army career, particularly as he learned the hard lessons of being a good messmate and a dependable officer. One of his observations goes directly to the importance of a service reputation and its relationship to performance: "The regiment did nothing overt to improve my character; it left that to me, giving me only good and bad examples and leaving me to draw my own conclusions. And I saw that ability was not really very important. It was for the conscientious, thoughtful, brave, and above all, straightforward man that people gave their best."[1]

One does not have to accept his assessment on the lesser importance of professional ability to benefit from his penetrating insight as to how character affects reputation. Think of professional reputation as a matrix. On one dimension are people who know you: officers who are retired, active duty seniors, contemporaries, and juniors. The other dimension is time: when you were a midshipman or at Officer Candidates School (OCS), a junior officer, a senior officer, and today at whatever rank you hold. Each of the cells in this matrix contains people who taken together define your service reputation. You might do well in one cell or in one time period and not so well in others. None should be overlooked as you conduct a self-assessment.

It is particularly easy to overlook two groups, juniors and retired officers, but you do so at your professional peril. As for retired officers, bear in mind that some of them were probably your CO's boss at one time. In other cases they may remember your performance more clearly than some active duty officers. As for juniors, let us look at a few examples of how juniors' views feed back into the performance and fitness report loops.

Some years ago a senior ship skipper ran roughshod over his subordinates. He cared little for their respect, and this was reflected in their low opinion of him. His focus was on his boss, not the people who worked for him. But in due course two of his subordinates, adequate but not great officers, were assigned to the staffs of the skipper's bosses, one a type commander, the other a fleet operational commander. The reassigned officers occupied little-known but important billets on their respective staffs and made sure their previous skipper's reputation was made well known throughout the staffs and subtly to their respective admirals. For the rest of his tour the skipper was putting out fires and answering staff queries to the degree that his ship's performance and his reputation suffered.

In another case a carrier skipper had on board a senior chief petty officer who had his hand on the pulse of the ship's morale. That morale was very high. What the skipper did not know was that the senior chief was an old shipmate and friend of a four-star officer in the skipper's chain of command and communicated with the latter frequently. The senior chief sang the praises of the carrier skipper, and although no cause and effect could be proved, the skipper was picked early for flag rank.

To a lesser degree similar effects are possible through the retired community, many of whom are well plugged in to current Navy decision making at all levels. Senior officers sometimes ask retired officers for advice; thus to have your name mentioned favorably by a retired officer to an active duty officer can do a great deal of good. "I knew him when he was my chief engineer on USS *Neversail* and . . ."

Next to juniors and retired officers, the most overlooked cells of service reputation are those that apply to contemporaries. I have come to the view over many years that it is your reputation among your contemporaries that is decisive. Seniors, more often than we like, can size you up incorrectly, but in my experience your contemporaries almost never do so. My advice to senior officers in selecting a junior officer for assignment to their staff is to poll not just seniors for whom the candidate has worked but also the candidate's contemporaries. They will know how solid the officer is, whether the individual has an alcohol problem, whether the candidate is too slick by half, and so on.

The point of this discussion is that you cannot just rely on a one-dimensional perspective of service reputation. You must look across the board and across time. It is not enough to wish for your seniors to become successful and influential mentors; your contemporaries and juniors should be similarly blessed.

I am not suggesting here that you must butter up juniors and contemporaries—or seniors for that matter. Rather, you must treat people as shipmates and colleagues, not stepping stones. Later, after you have retired, some of your more touching experiences will include being approached by an old shipmate and thanked for a chewing out or a hammering at a disciplinary hearing years earlier, accompanied by a comment along the lines of "Thanks, I needed that." Mental toughness and honesty will guide you through those shoals. You are living dangerously if you dismiss the good opinion of juniors, contemporaries, and retired officers as unnecessary to your future success.

To sum up: your fitness reports tell only part of your story. The rest of the story, and often a crucial part, is your professional reputation. Although you are screened or promoted on your record, the path to success lies through the selection board. As we shall see, one or more of its members briefs your record to the board. At that time you are discussed, questions are asked, and appraisals are made in open forum by the board. A solid reputation will carry you far in those deliberations.

It is rare to have an officer's record go before a promotion or screening board and find that the officer or all of his former skippers are unknown to all of the board members. It is so rare that the unfortunate officer is sometimes referred to as the "mystery man (or woman)" when the record is briefed to the board. If "mystery man's" record is very good, and he is in the finals, a board member might make discrete inquiries among his friends to get more information.

Your reputation starts building when you are a midshipman or officer candidate.

You will find that most early mistakes are overlooked with the passage of time. Your seniors, contemporaries, and juniors refine their assessments over time. What do you want them to say about you at cocktail parties, in selection and screening board proceedings, and in conversations with your future boss? Just as professional performance is built block by block, so too is your reputation. Some officers find that their professional reputation overwhelms their fitness report jacket come selection or screening board time. Sometimes a good selection board jacket is defeated by reputation. On the other hand, it is rare to have a good reputation outweigh a spotty selection board jacket. In those cases, however, the officer concerned will probably receive a close look by the board members as they try to sort through conflicting evidence of the officer's fitness.

There is an added but not central benefit to a good service reputation. When you do retire, you will carry your service reputation with you. If you have a good reputation, you will be a welcome addition to ship or squadron reunions. You have joined a band of brothers and sisters as you relive the exploits of your youth. At such times your reputation becomes even more precious. But there is more. You will find that your postservice employers in civilian life will also be interested in your reputation. They do not have access to your fitness reports. In ways that will seem mysterious, your prospective employer has his or her own sources to plumb your reputation during your service years. In some cases such inputs have been crucial—for good and ill—to the employment decision.

The lesson for junior officers is this. Do not for a minute think that your service reputation is unimportant—even if you are planning to leave the service at your first opportunity. Your service experience will add up to four to six years of your life. You will form or firm up habits during that period that will last a lifetime both in service and beyond. Future employers will be intensely curious about what you did and how well. Many will not accept a four- to six-year gap in your resume without some fill-in details. You should view each and every one of your bosses as a person who someday may be asked to comment on your service performance. How would you like to be remembered?

In the next chapter we discuss a group that is often a source of good career advice and essential to your good service reputation: sponsors and mentors.

4

Mentors and Cliques

Mentor: Trusted counselor or guide
—*Webster's New Collegiate Dictionary*

Mentoring involves a senior-junior relationship based on friendship, advice, and mutual respect and in some cases an extension of influence on the part of the senior. In the naval service this relationship has always been informal. There are indications, however, that this long-standing practice is receiving some official Navy support.[1] At their best, mentors provide a channel of career advice from an interested senior to a junior. At worst, mentoring may involve a senior using influence to gain some preferment (assignment or selection) for the junior outside the system.

Mentors can enhance their protégé's service reputation in a variety of ways. For example, in their conversations with other seniors officers, mentors might mention something about their protégé's superior performance. This information might be particularly useful to those seniors shopping to fill an important billet on their staffs.[2] Since the 1970s I have rarely seen or heard of direct interventions by mentors in the assignment system or promotion systems (the former is unprofessional, and the latter is illegal). I am not suggesting that senior officers have not asked for specific individuals by name to be assigned to their command. Most influence involves passing the word on the good qualities of a protégé. In that sense it is a positive component of one's service reputation. Nevertheless, some believe this type of mentoring is a form of political influence. I see it otherwise. Service reputation is a fact of life, and it is naïve to suggest that it be eliminated from the most sensitive decisions the Navy makes, that is, officer assignments and promotions.

In my experience the most valuable service a mentor can provide is career advice.

This advice goes far beyond such matters as future assignments. It includes guidance and suggestions on how to perform in staff and command functions, setting an example for the junior to emulate, pointing out the pitfalls and opportunities as one progresses in a naval career, and exposing the protégé to the real Navy that lies beyond the command's paperwork. Let us look at a historical example.

At one time the Naval Academy had an informal practice that assigned each plebe (a freshman) his own first classman (senior). The purpose was to provide the plebe personal instruction and mentoring outside the chain of command. The first classman "spooned" the plebe. That is, he put their relationship on a first-name, informal basis. The routine went like this. Before every meal formation the plebe would go to the first classman's room and provide some minor services: brush off his uniform jacket, report on the menu for the coming meal, and so on. The first classman in this relaxed setting would then proceed to inquire how the plebe was progressing in "learning his rates" (required plebe knowledge) on which he would be quizzed by other upperclassmen during the meal. He would also tell the plebe how he should improve his performance and demeanor. He would informally inspect the plebe's uniform and turnout. He would tell him how his classmates viewed the plebe's progress (or lack thereof). This casual but honest give-and-take helped junior midshipmen immensely and was a relief from the more formal dressings down a plebe routinely received from upperclassmen in general.

I will not forget the help I received from this system as I transitioned to the Navy's way of doing things. It was a senior-junior relationship—

but leavened with a dash of friendship against a backdrop of shared objectives (improving my performance). No favoritism was ever shown. Another good feature of the system was that each midshipman had his own first classman. No plebe, no matter how backward, was frozen out of the system.

In today's environment one does not go out and seek a mentor. A mentor picks you; you do not pick him or her. It is not a contract and is rarely mentioned in specific terms. A mentor usually picks you because that individual sees some promise in you and wants to help you realize it. It is an extension of friendship in the professional realm—and, like friendship, it has to this point stayed informal. In fact, the word "mentor" is rarely used. You might hear a senior say, "He is one of my boys," "I have been following her career closely," "He bears watching," or "She has great potential." Or a junior may jocularly refer to his mentor as his "sea daddy" in his conversations with his contemporaries.

All well and good, you say, but can I be more proactive in coming to the attention of senior officers and thereby obtain some of the benefits of having a mentor? This is wrong thinking. There are no shortcuts, and you must not campaign for such a relationship. The good news is that you do have one powerful tool at your disposal: *outstanding performance in your current job.* You will come to the attention of both your commanding officer and other potential mentors if you are demonstrating superlative performance. The word spreads quickly. If you see the mentor's role as helping you circumvent the rigors of the promotion and assignment systems (and the performance component that is the key input to them), you are on the wrong track.

You may ask for an example of how the mentor's advisory function works in practice. Some years ago there was an officer who, as a middling senior captain, had just become eligible for early flag selection. He was not yet in the flag selection zone, and a mentor of his served on the flag selection board. He was not selected on that occasion and probably deservedly so. But his mentor, although not compromising the secrecy of the promotion board, counseled patience and indicated the officer's strengths and weaknesses in the selection process. The mentor had seen the captain's entire record and was able to give him a very valuable assessment as to how he stacked up. His advice and counsel were of great benefit to the captain, and two assignments and two years later he was selected when he again came before the flag board. It is this advisory role and "spreading the word" role that best defines mentoring, rather than the exercise of favoritism—that favorite whipping boy of some who have experienced career disappointments.

What advice can I offer on the subject? If you are a senior, proceed on the basis of advice and see if it grows into a relationship based on mutual respect and friendship. Do not try to circumvent the existing systems to favor the friend. As a junior, mentoring will or will not come to you. If it does come to you, be careful not to abuse a confidence or friendship or seek preferment outside existing systems (the word gets out). *Your best mentor is your commanding officer because that officer has official levers with which to help and counsel you.* Commanding officers can talk to detail and placement officers, and they sign your fitness reports. They know your strengths and weaknesses and can advise you based on a factual observation of your performance. In fact, many mentorships start out as skipper–junior officer relationships (see chapter 2).

Cliques

There is a special—and rare in my experience—type of mentorship or collegiality that is inimical to good order and discipline: cliques. It is probably impossible to stamp out every abuse in mentorship and cronyism in any organization. Unfortunately, the histories of the armed services, including the Navy, suggest instances where a small group of officers may have attempted to manipulate the promotion and assignment systems to the advantage of themselves and favored colleagues. In some cases such cronyism was defended as advancing the good of the service. It was rarely overtly venal or self-serving. Indeed, the usual rationale for group cohesion was based on loyalty and forming a "team" or informal association to achieve some worthwhile end. Unfortunately, carrying interpersonal loyalty and team building in the extreme works against the larger officer population who are not included among the "in-groups."

In the early 1970s when Admiral Elmo Zumwalt was the Chief of Naval Operations some officers and even members of Congress charged that he was subverting the chain of command and giving preferment or special access to former shipmates and friends. In the admiral's defense, those years were demanding ones as the Navy went through major changes near the end of the Vietnam War. It is not surprising that he would install supporters of his vision of needed change in key positions in the Navy, particularly if he believed that strong institutional interests were working against it. But sometimes the best of motives carry one too far, and fairness and equity are sacrificed to achieve an objective.

A somewhat similar situation occurred in the early 1980s when John Lehman was Secretary of the Navy. Lehman, perhaps the strongest secretary since Teddy Roosevelt, worked diligently to install "his boys" in key positions. There is a lesson in all this for any serving officer: there are pitfalls in hitching your wagon to a single star. Some of Zumwalt's and Lehman's proteges suffered career setbacks when their mentor and sponsor left the scene. Your loyalty to the Navy should not be confused with loyalty to an individual, no matter how strong, charismatic, and influential he or she may be. You will find that the temptation to catch the tide may be too strong to be resisted. The key is to keep your perspective and balance and to hold the enthusiasms of the present in check.

Also resist the temptation to extrapolate from a few past real or perceived abuses of the mentoring system to a conclusion that you have been unfairly treated. It is but a small step from that comfortable notion to a conclusion that therein lies the explanation for your failure to screen or get promoted. My advice is to not worry about mentorship or the effects of politics or cliques. If a senior officer offers friendship and gives advice, take it as a gesture of friendship. But avoid being labeled a political officer or being seen as pulling strings for preferment. It will hurt your professional reputation. You will run across some officers who boast or subtly hint of having influence in high places so they can angle for an assignment they want or get a change of orders to suit their preference. What you are really seeing is a career in the process of being destroyed.

The Naval Academy Connection

Much has been made over the years about the supposed bonding that Naval Academy graduates enjoy and the assumed advantages they have over officers commissioned from other sources. Some of this criticism loses its punch when one considers that two of the last three CNOs have not been Naval Academy graduates. At one time in recent years neither the CNO nor the Vice Chief was a Naval Academy graduate.

Let me be clear here: we have a Naval Academy for a reason—to produce career officers and leaders for the nation and to set the standard for officer-producing systems throughout the service. The facts show that Naval Academy graduates have a higher career retention rate than do graduates of other commissioning programs. That is not the same as saying that other systems produce less-qualified officers. Nor is it to say that Naval Academy graduates enjoy a head start that benefits them throughout their careers. Nor is it to say that Naval Academy graduates are not proud alumni who have a bond of shared experience with other graduates. It is to say that a Naval Academy education provides a head start for fledgling officers so that they can hit the deck running if they apply themselves. Whether they keep that advantage over their non–Naval Academy peers is something they decide by the caliber of their performance in the fleet in the years that follow. Some Naval Academy graduates keep that edge, and some do not and may be resting on their laurels gained as midshipmen at the Naval Academy.

There is one special advantage—not crucial, but important—of a Naval Academy education. While midshipmen are at the Naval Academy, they come into contact with seven classes of midshipmen (their own class when they enter the academy, the three classes in front of them, and the three classes that follow as they progress). They graduate in sequence and then march through their careers together. It follows that graduates know the strengths and weaknesses of a large part of the officer corps at any given time starting with their own commissioning. They enter the fleet with a very large professional acquaintance among their contemporaries. This translates to the fact that their professional reputations, for good or ill, are more widely known in the service than those of their non–Naval Academy contemporaries. Almost as important is the fact that the Naval Academy's staff and military professors are heavily weighted with Naval Academy graduates. Hence, midshipmen at the Naval Academy graduate with an exposure to a large number of graduates beyond their own or adjacent-year groups. This acquaintanceship results more in added knowledge than in any basis for preferment among graduates.

Although the Naval Academy provides excellent preparation for lifelong service in the naval profession, it demonstrably is not the only way for professional success and the promotions that go with it. I have served with, under, and over officers from all accession sources. It would never occur to me, or anybody I know, to give preferment to Naval Academy graduates simply because they were graduates of that institution. Any skipper wants the best people regardless of commissioning source. To imply that there is some "canoe club" or "boat school" or "ring knocker" service mentality that stands in the way of promotion of nongraduates is to my mind pure rubbish. Although it may have had some basis up to and through World War II, that practice has long been dead. The Navy has changed from being led by a force of some five thousand

Naval Academy–trained officers in the 1930s to one of more than fifty thousand officers from a variety of commissioning sources today. Even if it wanted to, the Naval Academy cannot supply all or even most of the service's officer needs.

Do not focus on any initial edge that a Naval Academy graduate may have on commissioning. Hard work and good performance will make anyone competitive regardless of the commissioning source.

5

The Wardroom and
Ready Room Menagerie

Menagerie: A group or collection of persons that are strange, odd,
or foreign to one's expectations.
—*Webster's Third New International Dictionary*

Wouk writes about more oddball officers on a single ship than I
met in a lifetime of naval service.
—A senior admiral commenting on Herman Wouk's *The Caine Mutiny*

It is time in this narrative to lighten up a bit. Senior readers may want to skip
this chapter because they have heard or seen it all before. For the midshipmen and junior officers who remain, what follows is a series of caricatures of
officers with significant flaws in their attitudes and performance. You have
already encountered some midshipmen or cadets who at least in part fit these
descriptions. A few of them have gone on to get a commission. The service
does not have a lot of oddballs because most are winnowed out in the commissioning programs, and the remainder rarely last long in the fleet. Senior
oddballs are stock figures and the centerpiece of much naval fiction but a rar-
ity in the fleet I know. There seem to be more of them because the few who
exist receive an inordinate amount of attention and become well known in
the service. Avoid extrapolating from the actual few to the perceived many.

To this point in the book I have emphasized what you should do,
not what you should avoid. In this chapter I continue to emphasize

professional performance but reverse the perspective and present sketches that serve as cautionary tales. In most cases these culprits are self-absorbed officers who are having difficulty relating their performance and demeanor to their unit's mission. You may be sure that they will be the object of much counseling. Some so counseled turn the corner and perform well in the service after a difficult apprenticeship.

You will observe that more than 90 to 95 percent of the Navy's officers are hard-working, goal-oriented performers who are good shipmates. But there are limits to how many officers can be above average by any relative standard. The saving factor is that by any absolute standard, probably two-thirds of the officers in any group are excellent. Most will not qualify as future CNOs—whatever their spouses say—but they will be competent watch standers, division officers, ship handlers, and aviators. As for the remaining 5 to 10 percent, you probably would not depend on them in a pinch or welcome them as members of the family. Some of them are your competitors in the career race. Some of them are very able indeed.

Wardroom Lizards

Many years ago a popular descriptive term was "wardroom lizard." Wardroom lizards are officers who spend most of their time in the wardroom drinking coffee, shooting the breeze, reading magazines, or even taking a nap. They are rarely out on the deck plates seeing what is going on in their division. The good part of this situation is that their division chief or one of their Sailors with a chit to get signed knows where to find them when needed. By the way, speaking of signing papers, you will soon observe that much of the paperwork on a small ship or squadron gets done in the wardroom or ready room. Either no department office exists, or it is so small there is scant room for a junior officer. You have already found out that your stateroom aboard ship is unspeakably small. It is not uncommon to see working papers laid out on the wardroom's table cover and an officer hard at work going over official documents or

working with a laptop. These folks are not wardroom lizards; they are trying to get the unit's work done.

The aviation equivalent of wardroom lizards are the squadron mates who
believe they came into the Navy only to fly airplanes and that their ground
duties are best left to the chief—or department head. When ashore, these officers also seem to be absent a great deal—running errands to the nearby
exchange, picking up a latte at the nearby "roach coach," or kicking back in
the ready room looking at CNN or rolling the dice in an acey-deucey game.

You will often be so busy in your naval career you may believe there is
never enough time to do what needs to be done. Still, there are lulls when
there is time to catch up. Use this time effectively to improve your professional performance: get to know your equipment and spaces better, get to
know your enlisted people better, and ensure your time is fully invested just
like your money. Do not get the reputation as a lounger, an officer who is
more comfortable at idling speed than at cruising or top speed.

High RPM and Low Torque

Some officers do stay very busy, at cruising or top speed. But the unfortunate
fact is that they are all RPM—but low output. They give the appearance of
staying busy, dashing about or with a handful of papers in their hands—and
worried looks on their faces. But for some reason they do not seem to get
anything tangible done. Unfortunately, there is a great deal of administrative
work in the peacetime Navy. If you are not careful, it will cloud your judgment. Never forget why you are a naval officer: to be able to operate your ship
or squadron effectively in combat. The paperwork has to get done—and it
will be done. And you must do your share. But if most of your working day
is spent shuffling papers and responding to administrative crises, you (and
perhaps your boss) are losing sight of the object of the exercise.

Set aside part of your workday to learn, refresh yourself, and educate
yourself for combat. If war were to come to your ship or squadron tomorrow, how would your work priorities change? One of the reviewers of

an early draft of this book wrote: "One successful officer made a habit of writing short memos to himself every time he faced a curious or problematic situation as he progressed through the career wickets. Then, when he finally became a carrier group commander he put those personal 'lessons learned' into a guide for aircraft carrier commanding officers. It became a best seller."[1]

You need to maintain what aviators call "situational awareness." That is, you need to know how your personal and work environments relate to the big picture, mentally prioritize what you must do, and be very sensitive to changes. True, your work priorities are largely determined by your bosses, but there remains a wedge of time and mental capability under your personal purview. Invest those precious assets wisely.

Moaners

Some officers personify doom and gloom. The unit is going to hell in a handbasket, the senior officers do not know what they are doing, and "this old bucket will fall apart if they don't start paying attention." A variant of the moaners are the whiners or complainers.[2] It does not take these types long to deflect their negative outlook upward through the chain of command. The implication is that they are the only ones who know what is really going on—and that others do not know or do not care. These officers never met a job, a mission, a boss, or a cruise that they liked and respected. My advice: stay away from them. Most are past converting to a more positive outlook. In future years they will be moaning about why they were not selected or why they were denied the good jobs. If cornered by one of these types, ask them what they have done today to make things better. Then ask them to go on and tell you how they would do things differently as skipper. When cornered on this, they will shift fire to their skipper's boss or anyone else on which to lay the blame beyond themselves and to keep one person between them and the problem.

A variant of moaners are the officers who severely criticize their subordinates. They seem bemused by their difficulties and are puzzled when asked what their responsibility is for the chaos that swirls around them. These officers live on an island, incompetence above them and beneath them as they sail into the sunset and their first failure before a promotion board.

Moralists

In this section I am not talking about personal morals and the Ten Commandments. I am discussing those officers who see compromise as the work of the devil. They will stubbornly hew to a position or attitude because, in their words, "It is right." These officers cavil at every demonstration of flexibility or compromise entered into by their bosses to get the job done. Doctrinal or administrative purity is more important than the mission. They pose the false choice that "I would rather be right and passed over than wrong and promoted." A stubborn, inflexible, and self-righteous mind-set defines this officer type. They can be a real pain for those who are trying to get the job done and recognize that there is more than one way to do it.

This officer type is difficult to deal with. Most skippers give them the jobs that require the least suppleness of mind and are most closely defined by the regulations. As a result they themselves are responsible for the stunting of their professional growth. They are most comfortable when operating in a well-defined world and will be ill prepared for the rigors and uncertainties of combat. One mark of a maturing officer is gaining an understanding of the relationship between the enduring virtues and flexibility of mind and their effects on one's conduct.

Opportunists

Opportunism is not necessarily a vice. It depends on how it is used. "Striking while the iron is hot," "Time and tide wait for no man," "A window of opportunity," and "The time is right," are all useful admonitions and descriptors. But some individuals exploit opportunity for personal gain and preferment. When they justify an action, you must look carefully for the hidden message. They are slippery, looking for their chance, and often found to be rooting around in the debris of life's little disasters or periods of chaos. For example, they are quick to see a trip that is justified on the basis of government business as an opportunity to get a little personal business done at the same time. They see social occasions as opportunities to grind a personal axe with the boss. They see an opportunity to jump in and offer services when a colleague has faltered. In short, they are motivated by self-interest, and in their eyes the mission of the command and its officers is to help them achieve their own objectives. These officers tend to be quick-witted and often are very able. They are dangerous competitors in the face of gullible bosses. Your response to such "ambulance chasing" officers must be predicated on strength and respect, not weakness and venality. Do not cultivate them but do not accept their self-serving arguments, either. Keep them at a distance and in some doubt as to your power and influence.

Gossips

Gossip and loose talk are not military virtues, but many officers do not seem to recognize that simple fact. In an earlier era, gossip was considered "unmanly." Today it is unprofessional. Of course some officers in every unit keep their ears very close to the ground. Little goes on in the command that they do not know. Their pastime is exchanging tidbits with other like-minded souls. They do little harm in most cases, but they foster an atmosphere of greater reserve in social interactions. There is a prevalent fear that private matters will enter the public domain. This is particularly true in the case of misfortunes—who stumbled and why.

Closely akin to gossip is loose talk. In this kind of conversation, derogatory information is presented with only a casual regard for—and perhaps ignorance of—the facts. The message is considered more important than its factual basis. But one of the characteristics of your reputation that should be most treasured is that you speak from facts or when necessary identify assertions as opinions or allegations. One of the least complimentary things to be said about an officer is that the person acts before thinking, jumps to conclusions, or does not have the facts right.

Marshall Lyautey, a famous French colonial administrator and army officer, constantly worried about having "the trowel turn in my hand." He was referring to officers whose words could not be counted on as fact or who could not be depended on when hard decisions had to be made. He wanted trowels that did not turn and officers who were rock solid when they advised him.

Cool Hand Lukes

Some wardrooms or ready rooms have an officer who might be called a "Cool Hand Luke"—or Lucinda. Lukes are officers who are seemingly unperturbed by what is going on around them, have a sardonic detachment from the affairs of the command, seem always to land on their feet, and stay at some remove from daily problems and concerns. Officers who are closer to the action and suffer the "slings and arrows of outrageous fortune" often admire these individuals. Cool Hand Lukes seemingly do not care whether the command sinks or swims or succeeds or fails so long as events leave them alone to laugh at lesser mortals embroiled in the fray.

Ordinarily, Cool Hand Lukes are not a problem—except when they become ringleaders for officers who want to emulate them. If enough officers take on these individuals' attitudes, the ship or squadron starts to lose its cohesion. The skipper or XO who is not alert soon finds that a new power center has been created outside the chain of command. Cliques form, and some are left out—including some of the most diligent and responsible (but perhaps socially inept) officers in the command.

Cool Hand Lukes have not bought into the unit's mission and their role in it. Their seeming indifference is their armor. They purport to not be interested in promotion—and therefore are unlikely to be competitors in your career. It is not your job to save the Lukes from themselves, but you should be wary of their seductive charm in luring the less sophisticated to their banner.

Life-of-the-Party Officers

For life-of-the-party officers, wardroom and ready room life revolves around partying and horseplay. They are in the forefront of every wild idea, caper, spree, or overseas liberty. Their natural habitat is the "admin" of the unit in every liberty port. If there is no admin they establish an informal meeting and partying point. Life-of-the-party individuals have most of the organizing and leadership skills needed in a naval officer, leavened with an irreverent sense of humor. They are fun to be around but in many cases badly needing a rudder to keep them on course.

Their stock-in-trade is the well-placed jibe, the apt phrase, a poke in the ribs, and the riotous take-off on the characteristics of their seniors and more vulnerable contemporaries. Everybody seems to know them—and their reputation goes beyond the command. Most need a good solid dose of maturity. As a junior officer, do not mistake life-of-the-party officers as solid performers. Enjoy their company now because they likely will not be around for a full career.

Loners

The Navy is a sociable service. For the most part, naval officers and their families enjoy each other's company. The reason for this is shared experiences, often under difficult conditions, and the comradeship that comes from a mission that is larger than any one individual. But there is something more—a sense of loyalty that seems to grow up from the deck plates. Good officers—and most are—and their families help one another.

But some officers are loners. They enjoy their own company more than that of their shipmates. The possible reasons for this separateness are many. Some are just shy and afraid of rebuke. They are uncomfortable in interpersonal relations. Perhaps they are awkward or physically unattractive. Others are so wrapped up in their own personal interests that they do not have or make time for community and command interests. They show up and contribute and then go home and are not seen again until quarters the next morning. They keep their own counsel (not bad in itself) and often have to be prodded to become involved with group professional matters. Still others are bookish—introverted scholars whose interests are on an entirely different plane than those of their shipmates.

A subspecies of the loner type is particularly difficult to deal with: officers who are loners not because of any fear or concern but because they feel superior to their shipmates. At bottom they do not want to be in the command and are determined to have as little to do with it as is humanly possible. These loners sometimes transmorph into Cool Hand Lukes but more often are considered snobs rather than cool. In some cases the spouse is the source of the problem, particularly if that individual comes from a highly religious background or from a very wealthy or otherwise prominent family and considers the social life of the wardroom or ready room unworthy. There is no all-purpose answer to the problem posed by this type of loner. In most cases they are worth encouraging to participate in the mainstream of unit social life.

As a junior officer you have two obligations in this realm. First, do not become or be seen as a loner. Make the effort to become involved in the social life of the command. Take every opportunity to interact with your shipmates in both the professional and social spheres. This is not always easy, and you must be prepared for some rebuffs, but the effort is what counts, and you will likely see that effort reciprocated. I have found most naval officers to be outgoing. They enjoy comradeship, like to have a good time, and have a sense of humor. They will take it as a matter of pride to draw you out if you are experiencing difficulties in adjusting to the service. For most their first response is to be inclusive rather than exclusive.

Your second obligation is the mirror image of the first: help those who are having trouble making the adjustment to wardroom or ready room comradeship. Making that extra effort pays enormous dividends not only for your new friend but also for your own self-confidence in being able to interact effectively with people who are less self-confident that you are.

6

Spring Training

Chance favors the prepared mind.
—Louis Pasteur

In February and March of each year, the attention of baseball fans is drawn toward Florida and Arizona as favorite teams undertake spring training and getting prepared for the upcoming baseball season. At this time players hone the skills needed to survive a season that for some does not end until the following October. Getting physically and mentally in shape for an uncertain future is not limited to ballplayers, however. For naval officers, spring training is a year-round activity: getting ready for the next hurdle and the challenges of leadership in an environment where the stakes are much higher than on the baseball diamond.

How do you prepare yourself to achieve good performance and, ultimately, promotion? A better question is how do you prepare yourself to perform at a higher level? The answer reads like a laundry list. Achieving some of the skills needed requires—surprise!—hard work and continued application. In this chapter, I discuss some techniques you may have overlooked.

Mentally Fleeting Up

"Fleeting up" is a time-honored Navy term that describes taking over your boss's job when that individual is not there. But the fleeting-up concept is also a useful technique for preparing yourself for command. Using this method, you simply contemplate the decision your boss is called on to make and then mentally put yourself in that individual's place and work the problem through to a solution. This is not the time for glib comments or horseback guesses. Do not take the easy path. Unfortunately, there are no simple answers to the major problems of command.

A variant of this technique is to assume your boss has become incapacitated and that now it is up to you to make the necessary decisions. Imagine that your professional reputation rests on the decision. You must act! This vicarious mode of decision making and learning will expand your mind, and you will grow both in situational awareness and in preparedness. What would be your agenda if you suddenly had to represent your ship or squadron in discussions with your skipper's commodore or air wing commander (CAG)? Put aside the conventional wisdom of your junior officer buddies. For the moment, even if only in your mind, assume you are wearing your boss's stripes and that what you do will have a major influence on your command. Have you done the hard preparatory work—spring training—of marshalling the facts and working the problem? Why not go a step further and put the results into your computer?

And here is a suggestion for skippers: give your XO and department heads the day off and tell your junior officers that they will fill the temporarily vacant positions for the day (let your commodore or CAG know what is going on). Your junior officers should prepare and sign off on the plan of the day, the flight schedule, and messages that must be sent. If this prospect worries you, you should ask yourself what you are doing to prepare them to fill the gaps when necessity arises. When the first team returns, call a wardroom/ready room meeting and ask how your junior officers improved on the example their seniors have set. This exercise can be a lot of fun, and it also gives you and them an opportunity to make some serious points from which all can benefit.

Focusing on Where Your Command Needs the Most Help

Adm. Ernest King, the Navy's CNO during World War II, once remarked, "'Difficulties' is the name given to things it is our business to overcome."[1] As you look around you, what are your command's "difficulties" or problems? What can be done about them? What can you do to help your department head or skipper? Look at problems as a puzzle to be solved, not a difficulty to be avoided. I suggest that you put a list of such problems on your computer and keep a running commentary on solutions—those you offer mentally and those that are actually effected by your bosses. Add paste-up notes along the way to document your reasoning and the factors involved.

For example, let us suppose your command has a shortage of personnel in a few important ratings. Consider the command's billet structure and how it is manned (what the command is allowed and what it has on board). Add in when more personnel are expected. Ask yourself what levers the command has to gain improvement. What work-arounds are available? What messages would you send, and what discussions would you have with your commodore or air wing commander or the Naval Personnel Command? How would you make the onboard personnel more effective? What will be the effects if the shortfall is not remedied before deployment? Or, to expand your examination further afield, why is that rating so chronically undermanned? What are the selective reenlistment bonus (SRB) or special pay levels? How can the Navy offer more than the civilian job market?

Speaking Up

Are you taking advantage of every opportunity to polish your public speaking skills? One such opportunity is holding training sessions with your division. Surely you know something that they need to know to do well on promotion exams. If you avoid opportunities to hone your communications skills before an audience, you are postponing the inevitable. If you aspire to command, you will be required to speak in public and speak well.

One skipper I knew had the remarkable ability to gather the squadron's crew around him on the hanger deck, mount a chair as a makeshift rostrum, put the crew at ease, and tell them what was on his mind. He would discuss what the squadron faced in an upcoming deployment by laying out the problems the officers and crew had to solve with him, asking for their ideas, explaining why the workday had to be extended temporarily, and so on. His talent as a speaker and his ability to make eye contact with every Sailor in the squadron had an electrifying effect. Problems seemed to fall away or at least seem easier. His department heads saw command leadership in action. American Sailors will do almost anything for you if you level with them, treat them with the respect due shipmates, and make them part of the solution. This technique has served many officers well throughout their careers.

Like so many other good things, however, speaking well takes work and practice. Clearly the skipper just mentioned had considered what he wanted to say and how he would say it. Could you make the equivalent effort to speak to your division or department if the need arose? What would you say to them?

Knowing the Most about the Systems

Who in your unit knows the most about the systems under your cognizance? Your first answer to this question is probably your chief petty officer, which is an understandable response, particularly if you have not been aboard very long. *But how far down the enlisted rate structure in your division do you have to go before your knowledge is on a par?* When you determine that level, ask yourself what added value *you* contribute to your division's "product." Have you ever studied the advancement in rate manuals that apply to the ratings in your division? Could you pass the exam? If not, why? Do you see your role as solely an officer in training and, hence, excused from the need to acquire concrete and fundamental knowledge of the system? If you do see your role that way, when do you believe that circumstance will change? If you remain unconcerned about the details of the work under your cognizance, you will not make it—not in the Navy and not in civilian life. There is no easy path from where you stand today to achieving an intimate knowledge of the content of the job and ultimately becoming an executive or leader who can instruct others. The ladder upward is slippery, and each rung on that way up is hard earned and easily measured.

The tenor and content of these questions and comments should suggest to you that you need to be hands-on with what is going on in the division or in matters under your cognizance. Skating along and excuses ("Let the chief do it") are easy. Ambitious officers who are preparing themselves for command eschew the easy way and are hands-on performers who know their "stuff." This does *not* mean that you do the chief's work for that individual. Chiefs have their jobs to do, and you should stay out of their business (business that usually centers on the "how," not the "what" or "when"). But basic professional competence is both their business and yours.

Peace to War

How would your job (and your attitude toward it) change if we went to war tomorrow? I touched on this subject in an earlier chapter, but here I am addressing it in a "spring training" context. Considering this topic is another way of clearing out the peacetime cobwebs. So much of what we do in peacetime is oriented to administering, saving operating funds, taking care of our equipment, and training that we often overlook priorities directly related to war fighting. Suppose survival and war fighting took pride of place over your peacetime maintenance and training missions—and your prospects of advancement. This type of spring cleaning is occasionally needed in every command except those actually in combat or on the verge of deployment to a combat theater. Have you thought of proposing to your skipper that you orchestrate and direct an internal exercise for your unit to establish a war-fighting mind-set?

Focusing on Physical Fitness

To those who have been in combat, one of the most vivid memories is not fear but the physical exhaustion occasioned by long stretches of stress, anxiety, and uncertainty. We all have experienced (or will experience) the long periods on the bridge, in the cockpit, or in ready status on the catapult preparing a series of weapons launches, performing underway replenishments (unreps), and looking for the enemy while ensuring the unit stays in a high state of readiness. We have all had situations where at any moment we might have to give our best to survive and complete the mission.

Although there is a large portion of mental preparedness in this equation, physical readiness is of vital importance as well. Are you in shape? Can you function in an environment of long periods of sleep deprivation? Once you get out of shape, it becomes increasingly difficult with age to regain it. When you step on the bridge, go into combat, or drop in the cockpit, you should be rested and alert. But you must work to achieve the conditions that make it possible. Physical fitness is one of the best assets you can have in the professional performance sweepstakes. You need not be a jock—but you must have strength, stamina, and adequate rest. You need to manage your physical condition the same way you would manage any other asset. This means proper diet (when possible), the ability to catch catnaps on the fly during the rare interludes, and exercise.

Exercise means more than strength conditioning, although that is important. It also involves aerobic exercise to stress your cardiovascular system, keep your body pipes clean, and keep you alert. If you do not sweat, you are not working out. You also need to ensure that your range of motion is adequate, and that takes exercise also—stressing your arms, legs, torso, and neck in a disciplined way through the limits of your range. But the most important habit is to get into a regular *routine* of exercise— not crash courses to get back in shape. Your exercise regimen should be designed carefully so that you test and increase your limits without over-doing it; it should also be suitable for use aboard ship and ashore. You will not cross the career finish line at the top of your game unless you are in good shape. Nobody else can do it for you. Here is another tip: my seaman's eye tells me that nearly as many officers encounter health prob-lems as selection board problems as they become more senior. If your health becomes questionable because of diet or lack of exercise, so are your prospects for promotion.

Looking Fit

How do you look? Physical fitness is part of the answer to this question. You must look fit, and you will if you are fit. A round of golf every week simply will not do it. Do not mistake fun for fitness, although there is some overlap. Do your uniforms fit? If not, get in shape so that they do or get new uniforms. Do you look like an officer your subordinates would follow in battle? Is your uniform clean, pressed, and worn prop-erly? Many observers who do not know your hidden sterling profes-sional qualities will get their initial impression from your appearance in uniform.

Beyond physical condition and dress is the matter of personal demeanor. Many young people in civilian life seem to slouch, shuffle, or scuff their way from one point to another. Some find it difficult to main-tain eye contact. Others slur their words in imitation of the latest pop group performer or film star. For the new officer, most of these attributes are left behind plebe summer or during basic training in their OCS or

Naval Reserve Officers Training Corps (NROTC) unit. But over a lifetime you should pay attention to your posture, the habit of looking a questioner or conversation partner square in the eye, and speaking clearly and directly. If you look alert, involved, and decisive, you probably are, and you will find these attributes serve you well in watch standing and combat.

7

Do You Shine in
the Career Marketplace?

Good performance produces good assignments. High performers
don't really get a choice of assignments. On the other hand they get
choice assignments because of their high performance.
—Vice Adm. Robert F. Dunn USN (Ret.)

What is it that makes some officers so well known among their peers and
seniors? A few officers are tabbed as admiral material while still lieutenant
commanders and commanders. Some, probably with a bit of jealousy,
refer to them as "fair-haired boys," "water walkers," or "acolytes of the high
and mighty." Other highly regarded officers are spared such labels but
clearly and with some generosity of spirit are considered head and shoulders above their contemporaries. As a junior aviator I remember clearly
my seniors referring to the legendary admiral Jimmy Flatley as one such
individual. I recall hearing one flag officer remark that Adm. George
Anderson (a classmate of the speaker) was clearly marked as a future CNO
while still a captain. Adm. Tom Moorer had a similar reputation, and I
can still hear his contemporaries remarking in awe that he (an aviator)
made flag without ever having had command of a carrier—a necessity in
those days. Adm. Arleigh Burke went from two stars to become the CNO,
and few were surprised.

What is it that clearly marked these officers so early in their careers?
Each story has a different key element. Admiral Flatley was beloved by

his subordinates as a superb tactician, brilliant combat leader, and people-oriented commander. Admiral Anderson is remembered for his intellectual brilliance, his decisiveness, and his ability to get things done in tough environments. Admiral Moorer is still recognized as the towering naval figure of his era who did everything well that he turned his hand to. He was a greatly respected skipper and a tough-minded CNO and chairman of the Joint Chiefs of Staff when major decisions had to be made. Admiral Burke was a superb tactician, a man who instinctively saw the broader perspective; he held the CNO post for an unprecedented six years.

We cannot all have their skills, but we can learn from their performance. In looking over the careers of the officers identified early for future promise, the observer is struck by the fact that they all took on the tough jobs on the way up and did them well, so well that they came to the attention of the entire naval service. In some cases those jobs involved great political skill, but not political skill in terms of advancing themselves. Instead, they had skill in getting a high-visibility job done under the difficult conditions of working with other naval organizations or warfare specialties and other services. Later in their careers they worked just as skillfully with other organizations—Congress, the Joint Chiefs, or diplomatic representatives of the country's allies.

Characteristics of Comers

Now step back from the careers of a small number of legendary flag officers and look around you both within and outside your current command. Some of your contemporaries are already gaining recognition as being "head and shoulders" officers and are well known (at least by reputation) to you as "comers." What strikes you about their performance? Put luck aside. No one is lucky or unlucky for the twenty to twenty-two years it takes to make captain or to fail of selection one or more times. Some salient characteristics of these officers catch the eye.

When you consider your friends, contemporaries, and seniors who enjoy "comer" status, you will note some common characteristics that stand out. First, you would identify strength of intellect. Even if they are not the smartest people in the race for advancement, they are smart enough to learn quickly from their mistakes and those of others and to see how the lessons apply to often-unpredictable future situations. Intellectual acuity and suppleness are key virtues. And you will observe that some of that intellectual ability can be learned along the way. It is not a birthright.

Second, you might observe that they are decisive and have the ability to communicate their decisions and advice in such a way as to be compelling and persuasive to seniors and subordinates. Often this skill is acquired as a very junior officer. In short, they are courageous decision makers. They are not needless risk takers, but they know when and how to make a decision and disregard personal consequences. They sail close to the wind, but they are never becalmed. C. S. Forester, a great English naval novelist, had Adm. Lord Sir William Cornwallis cautioning a young Commander Horatio Hornblower: "But remember this. You'll find it hard to perform your duty unless you risk your ship. There's folly and there's foolhardiness on one side, and there are daring and calculation on the other. Make the right choice and I'll see you through any trouble that may ensue."[1]

Third, we would note that the emerging great leaders have the best kind of toughness, even ruthlessness, to make the correct decision regardless of personal consequences. Their critics may add that the ruthlessness sometimes extends to their desire to succeed at a personal level. But experience tells us that personally ruthless officers seldom succeed to high command, and when they do, they are heartily disliked and that that dislike feeds back into diminishing their personal reputation and eventually puts a cap on their aspirations.

The better form of ruthlessness puts the highest premium on moral integrity and mission accomplishment. The popular Hollywood stereotype of a very popular commander who puts the affection of his crew as his principal objective misses the mark, and he is not the person I want to lead me in combat. Subordinates prefer the commander who is successful as an operator and in combat. They will brag about this individual endlessly. They expect their skippers to be hard but fair. That phrase, "hard but fair," captures the essence of the mental and moral toughness that is so highly regarded.

One naval leader who carried such ruthlessness to near the extreme was Adm. Ernest J. King, the Chief of Naval Operations during World War II. King did not suffer fools gladly and had little time for friendship. His loyalty was to the service, not individuals. King was disliked by many, feared by some, but respected by almost all.

He had a tough job to do—picking up the pieces after a major naval defeat and going on to win a major war against tenacious and able enemies. One does not have to enjoy King's sundowner's reputation—that is, tough, strong-minded, and ruthless—but all can learn from his single-minded focus on the objective. He harshly pushed aside officers, some very senior, who did not measure up or who were unsuited for combat decision making even though they had scaled the promotion ladders of the peacetime Navy.

The Marketplace

The marketplace for naval officers is defined by the demand for the *best* officers and the small supply of those officers. Note the emphasis on the word *best*. Many good officers are available to fill billets, but understandably every skipper and shore boss wants the best. They want the best because they view their jobs as deserving the best and because if they have the best working for them, they will do a better job. The battles in the marketplace are joined wherever officer jackets for key positions are reviewed by shopping seniors, during flag-slating sessions conducted at the top levels of the Navy, and in the day-to-day interaction between placement and detail officers in the Navy Personnel Command. The battles are strongly fought, and at times the officer being considered becomes directly involved. Mostly the battle is fought by others with you as the prize. How do you shine in such a marketplace?

It almost goes without saying that the key elements of a top-notch promotion jacket are outstanding fitness reports, commendations, and other bouquets. This book is largely about how you should perform and ultimately field such a jacket. The second ingredient to competitiveness in the marketplace is your professional reputation. This becomes even more critical as you become more senior and the number of your active-duty contemporaries decreases. By the time you are a captain, and in some cases as a commander, you will be well known to those who have the biggest voice in your future.

But this record building begins in your present job. By the time you are more senior and have had a very successful major command tour as a captain, you are considered to be a contender for flag rank and are looked over very carefully in the assignment and placement process. You will find that your services are much sought after and that the detailers treat your next assignment very carefully.

A third component is your set of professional credentials. Have you had postgraduate education in the field related to the billet under consideration? For example, do you have a subspecialty in such areas as communications, computer management, or comptrollership? Have you served in joint or combined billets? Have you had a successful command tour? A perceptive insight into how your qualifications might play in the marketplace is set out in appendix B, where a former detailer shares his experience with you as to where the real demand lies.

The final element of your marketability is your experience. Do you have recent fleet experience? Have you proved yourself in tough jobs? Have you dealt with Congress, foreign officials, or the civilian departments of government? No one expects all of these credentials and experiences in a junior officer, but they do expect you to fill out your resume as you grow in seniority. You should have a shopping bag of skills that includes command at sea and a variety of tools earned in positions ashore. The question is not only how your fitness reports look in the marketplace but also what else you have to offer.

This is the proper place to introduce our next topic, your professional education and its place in your career development and in the market.

8

Been to School Lately?

At some point an officer who wishes to compete for flag rank *must* complete joint professional military education and a joint tour.

—A detailer commenting on the competing demands
  on an officer's time

The junior officer reader may be saying: "Whoa! I just got here. Flag rank is something that commanders and captains worry about." True, but if you stay for a career you will encounter the Navy's schoolhouse again, and the timing, duration, and content of that encounter can affect your performance, assignments, and promotions. Therefore, you should start thinking now about what you plan to do about furthering your education in the Navy. You still have time to decide, but thoughtful mental preparation is needed early in your career.

The Navy's schoolhouse is a controversial subject because various people hold strong but alternative views about how officers should spend their time in the face of competing demands in a fast-paced career. At one time the Navy was considered an anti-intellectual service. Many believed that a naval officer's natural school ground was the school of the ship, not the halls of academe. The old salts strongly resisted the establishment of the U.S. Naval Academy. The establishment of the Naval War College and the Naval Postgraduate School faced lesser but nonetheless similar opposition. That era seems to be behind us, but vestiges of those earlier times remain.

A Navy Education

Four major components make up the Navy's officer education programs: (1) undergraduate programs such as the Naval Academy and the NROTC system; (2) the Navy graduate education program at the Naval Postgraduate School and selected public and private universities; (3) many of the schools in the long training pipelines for officers going to sea billets where *education* is as important as *training*; and (4) professional military education (PME) at the Naval War College and the comparable war and staff college programs of the other services, the joint colleges, and the colleges of some of our international security partners. The discussion that follows centers on the last three components listed.

Postgraduate Education

As you read this chapter you have probably finished your commissioning pipeline and are in your first sea job. At some point in the next few years you will be assigned ashore, and you will be considered for assignment to a postgraduate education course at Monterey or a civilian university. The process involves your requesting a postgraduate course and being screened for it. At one time such screening was very rigorous and took into account your undergraduate education performance and your career potential. Most career-minded officers applied for such a course of instruction, and completing it successfully was a major milestone on a normal career path. Although an advanced degree is still a plus on your record and prepares you for assignment to an associated specialty billet, there are ample indications that it is not as essential as it once was. Fewer of the best officers seem to have time to spend at such schools, and there have been a few cases of academically successful students at the Postgraduate School failing of selection to lieutenant commander or commander.

The point of these observations is not to discourage you from seeking a two- to three-year postgraduate course. I only caution you that some risks are involved, risks that may be overlooked in the rush to get a degree or to return from sea to what is perceived as a less-demanding professional environment ashore. The risks include future assignment to a specialty only tenuously related to the postgraduate course attended, being away from your warfare specialty for too long, and having little time left for a professional military education program essential to your further career progress. It comes down to how you and your detailer work to use your scarce time and how much you like the hard work in the classroom.

The Sea Duty Pipeline

The Navy's leadership puts most of its attention and funding on imparting professional technical skills (many such skills have an education component), not on academic scholarship. Accordingly, more emphasis is placed on the officer training pipelines to the fleet than on graduate education programs. These pipelines include nuclear power training and refresher tours, replacement aircrew training, the various surface warfare schools, and assorted sea-oriented schools that prepare you directly for your fleet billet (e.g., engineering schools, catapult and arresting gear schools, missile courses, and the Prospective Commanding Officer [PCO] schools). The Navy has not made a conscious decision to trade off higher education for pipeline training, but the effect remains by default. It has not taken long for the message to get out to fleet wardrooms, ready rooms, and offices in the shore establishment. Most officers today want an advanced degree but see little time available to get it without risking a detour in their careers. Many pick up a degree while on shore duty (e.g., the Naval Academy's company officer degree program and the Naval War College degree program). If asked, many of these degree aspirants will frankly admit that they want the degree more for their postservice resume than for any direct benefit they might see during their naval service. As far as they are concerned, an advanced degree (particularly in a liberal arts or "soft" subject) is a plus for them, but not a key ingredient in the deliberations of a future selection board.

Many aviators rolling ashore want duty in the replacement air wing (RAG) rather than going to the Naval Air Training Command to instruct. Few seek Washington duty or assignment to the Postgraduate School. They want "hours in type" (that is, flight hours in a specific type of aircraft) to be more competitive for command screening when their time comes. Most officers in all warfare communities understandably want to stay close to their profession. It is where they can stay in touch and be evaluated by rising seniors, rather than get lost in the academic world and be out of sight and out of mind for as long as two to four years. Some senior aviators screened for nuclear power training for eventual command of an aircraft carrier worry about being away from their professional specialty for too long.

Professional Military Education
Attendance at a war college will improve your professional performance in that you will get a wider perspective of the naval profession and national security. It may not necessarily make you a better commanding officer of a fleet unit, but it will improve your performance as a staff officer in Washington and elsewhere and give you some of the intellectual underpinnings needed for high command.

After a long holiday (roughly 1945 to 1990) in which attendance at one of the many war and staff colleges was not essential to career progression, PME programs have returned to their previous importance. Attendance at a PME course is now essential for consideration for promotion to flag rank. But there are many ways to fill this requirement. There are long and short courses, and there are courses at the institutions of the other services. Moreover, there are qualifying correspondence courses for those who are particularly pressed for time and cannot squeeze in a residential course.

Although it is not anti-intellectual anymore, the naval service is faced with the realities of competing priorities that tend to push higher education aside.[1] Those competing priorities are an emphasis on youthful service leadership (compared to an earlier era), extended sea duty pipeline training, obligatory tour(s) in Washington and in joint duty, and the historical practice of highly valuing tours at sea (the longer the better).

Issues in Making a Decision

Submitting a future duty preference card for a tour in postgraduate education or at a war college is no longer the easy decision that it once was. It needs your careful consideration. The issues are as follows: Should you do it and, if so, when in your career? Do you have time in your career path? In what area or areas are you leaning? Do you stay in the school of hard knocks, or do you broaden your educational base and enhance your resume by going to one of the Navy's top schoolhouses?

Some years ago one officer had the choice of going to sea and working for a brilliant flag officer who was at the top of his profession or of going to Harvard Business School. He could not do both. He went to sea. Taking a longer view, he probably did the right thing because he worked for that flag officer two more times in his career and went on to flag rank. His choice might not be the best for you. These crossroads, where you have to choose, occur in every career. The easy choices are those that involve a good road and a less-than-best road. But when both roads are attractive, you will be put to the test.

One theory of career progression is that at most you have only one "throw-away tour" in a career. Your detailers will not like that phrase; to them every billet is important because they must fill it. In their view the assignment they have in mind will likely improve your future marketability, but in my view this is not necessarily true for the really top jobs. If my theory is correct, you need to select that tour very carefully. Perhaps postgraduate education is the answer. Perhaps you need an overseas tour or, if an aviator, a tour to fatten up your flight log. Overlaid on these decisions is the need to have some time with the family, to relax a bit from the pressures of sea duty, and to get your professional bearings. One surface warfare detailer cautions that "any low-impact job taken after a department head tour may prove impossible to overcome, as it comes by definition at the expense of something else that must be done (D.C. tour, War College, tough sea job to help with screen for XO or command)." He goes on to note that the surface Navy goes out of its way to offer every junior officer who commits to Department Head School a ticket to graduate education. The individual may go through the Naval Postgraduate School, degree programs at universities near naval operating bases and schools, or high-visibility programs (e.g., a master's degree in business administration or a politico-military master's program). Because more career "wickets" are involved, submariners and aviators have less latitude in making such choices.

Another option is to get advanced education on your own. Extension courses at a local university, War College correspondence courses, and other individual study opportunities are available. One former CNO encouraged officers to take this path if they were not interested in graduate education in the scientific and quantitative disciplines. Later CNOs, however, have held otherwise.

Most of the Navy's current postgraduate curricula are oriented to technical disciplines and future assignment to one of the several systems commands or laboratories or as prospective Naval Academy faculty. For many officers, these curricula also serve as stepping-stones into the restricted line (engineering duty, and aeronautical engineering duty in particular). Before applying for such a course, you must determine in your own mind that that is where you want to spend the critical years of your naval career. There is nothing wrong with that choice, and the Navy needs good officers in those jobs. But you should weigh your promotion and assignment opportunities and limitations when you select that path. So-called payback tours are the norm, and you will likely be assigned to one or two in your subsequent shore assignments.

If engineering is your first love after command at sea, by all means get the requisite postgraduate education and serve ashore in payback tours in one of the systems commands or related activities. The Navy needs some of its best senior and flag officers for responsible positions in each. But in my judgment your chances for assignment to most of the best jobs will be lower than if you had performed just as well in the various Pentagon staffs. I provide some additional treatment of the dilemmas in post-graduate education in appendix A.

Do It Yourself

A major factor in your school program should be self-study. You do not have to go to school to learn. Nor do you need to rely solely on experience to prepare yourself for what you will face downstream in a naval career. Much of your education is in your own capable hands. Correspondence courses are available, including some excellent ones sponsored by the various war colleges, but here I am talking about your self-directed professional reading. Thanks to the Naval Institute and other military publishers, some excellent books are available for instructing you in your duties and in your approach to your profession. But you need your own library. Do not rely solely or even partially on what you can check out of the base or ship library. Unless you are in a very large ship or on a very large base, you will not find all that you need in the library.

Therefore, you should start accumulating your own professional reference library—perhaps even before you are commissioned. I have seen personal professional naval officer libraries totaling more than three hundred works. Unless you are a bibliophile, that is more than you need. One or two dozen carefully selected books will do. Appendix C outlines a starter library for the newly commissioned officer. Most are "how-to" books akin to the one before you. You should also add the occasional naval history or biography to round out your education and your source material. Budget to buy a book every month or two. You might do well to start with the Naval Institute's book catalog. Their listing is comprehensive and not limited to books published in-house.

Your reading habits are important. You may find yourself overwhelmed with studying papers or official documents that are in your in-basket. You may be taking a postgraduate course of instruction, or you may be enrolled in a PME course with its own reading lists. Nevertheless, try to budget at least fifteen minutes a day (thirty is both reasonable and sufficient) to further your own professional education. Read through each book in your own professional library as you acquire it and then put it back on the shelf and return to it in a year or two for skimming and selective re-reading. You will find that during your career you will have extended periods of waiting for things to happen. Exploit every moment—whether it is waiting for the dentist, waiting for your spouse to get dressed, waiting for or traveling by plane, or waiting for your number to be called in a variety of circumstances. The discipline of reading is important. If all else fails, read at the breakfast table (assuming an understanding spouse, of course!).

Throw in some fiction occasionally. Some excellent naval fiction resides on the shelf alongside the potboilers. The best authors provide lessons to be learned vicariously. The works of Patrick O'Brian, C. S. Forester, William Mack, Ned Beach, and Marcus Goodrich come to mind. Do not waste time on books that bore you. Look for a better one on the same subject. Time is too short to read an author or material that does not fully engage you.

In the "old Navy," before we had war colleges and postgraduate courses, officers had to educate themselves. Indeed, even at the old Naval Academy, midshipmen were largely self-taught—but institutionally tested on their diligence and learning. Reading books (or manuals) is a time-tested way to self-improvement. Do not rely on spoon-feeding to get your education.

9

Sea/Shore Rotation and Homesteading

> The ramifications of the trend in officer assignment towards homesteading have not been fully digested by the Navy's leadership.
> —Former detailer

The entire Navy assignment system is built around rotation from sea duty to shore duty and back. This fact is driven both by the arithmetic of the numbers of sea and shore billets and by the need to have sea-seasoned officers in shore billets. A side benefit is to give officers a chance to broaden their career skills ashore. Following in importance is the desire to give officers a respite from the constant deployments and family separations inherent in most sea duty. Sea/shore rotation is a fact of life, and you try to change it at your professional peril. Long extensions on sea duty might be considered fun, and long extensions on shore duty may give you more time with your family, but either can throw your career progression off pace. If you extend on sea duty or overseas shore duty, it probably means that you are going from a ship or squadron to a staff or fleet support activity that is technically sea duty. If you extend (or are extended) ashore, it means you are being delayed in getting important sea qualifications.[1]

My advice is to accept rotation as an immutable pattern of life and plan accordingly. A not-so-subtle shift in this pattern occurs as you get more senior. When junior, the balance is tipped in favor of sea duty (again, the proportion of junior billets at sea and ashore drives this), and as you get more senior you will find that shore tours are longer and that sea tours become shorter. Fast-track aviator captains are an exception; often they will spend almost all their time in grade at sea. Nevertheless, by the time you are a captain and have twenty-four to twenty-five years of service, most of you can plan to spend the rest of your time ashore.[2] Plenty of jobs—most of them good—are available even if a flag is not in your future.

The temptation also exists to extend your tour at sea. After all, that is where the real action is. But one of the objectives in your career planning is balance. The possibility is real that the upcoming Washington tour will do more for your professional growth than an additional tour at sea—particularly if you go to a sea staff. If an extension at sea or shore means an early or additional command tour, by all means take it. But bonus commands are rare in these days of a smaller Navy.

Homesteading

You will hear the term "homesteading" often. It means that you get two or more back-to-back tours in different commands at the same location. You might go from sea to shore in the same city, such as Norfolk, San Diego, or Pearl Harbor, that is, wherever there is a concentration of naval activity. One detailer asserts:

> There is an undeniable trend towards homesteading in the surface Navy. Wardrooms filled with young, single, and highly mobile officers are gone. In their place, we find young married officers, married officers with many years of prior enlisted service, and officers married to other service members. We find officers with spouses who have demanding, rewarding jobs; we find officers who have older children—children who are more settled and more involved in community activities and less interested in moving every two years. For these reasons "ship type" has been bumped by "home port" as the number one priority on preference cards.[3]

If this assessment is correct, and the evidence suggests it is, the ramifications for career management and officer expectations are profound because it is rare to have two career-enhancing tours back to back in the same locality unless an individual is going from one command billet to another. The more frequent homesteading case is to "roll" from a good sea job to a lesser shore job. Ambitious officers cannot afford to spend any or much time in lesser jobs; in accepting them they incur the risk of future disappointment in the screening and assignment processes.

Exceptions exist, however. For example, you might roll out of your good sea billet in a unit homeported in Norfolk and be ordered to the Joint Forces Staff College, thereby buffing up your joint credentials. Or as a squadron skipper at Oceana you may be ordered to command a RAG squadron (as a bonus). Or you may be ordered to a good job on the staff of a real comer and have an opportunity to show what you can do before an appreciative potential mentor. But the exceptions need to be considered carefully. Sad but true, the odds are high that another tour in the same locality will not be the *best* career move. Detailers in many cases like homesteading because it saves them money out of their travel budget (always pressed), and often they can get you to your new duty station quicker (which is important if the billet is gapped or the officer you are relieving is badly needed somewhere else quickly). But your best interests are not always served by making it easy for detailers. Although they want to make you happy and more promotable, they also have a job to do—billets to fill quickly, travel funds to save, and so on. And they can always make a persuasive case for accepting the billet under consideration.

Often there are extenuating factors in homesteading: the kids are in good schools, the spouse has a well-paying job, you are a pillar of the church, you like the community, you are not ready for the Washington rat race, and so on. All are seemingly good reasons—but not good enough if you are serious about pressing on with your career, growing professionally, and buffing up your promotion board jacket. If the attractions of homesteading are great, you and your family are experiencing the first pangs of looking forward to your early retirement.

To sum up, if you are offered an opportunity to homestead where you are, find out what other transfer opportunities are available, opportunities that may entail a personal hardship but are more career enhancing. Good deals are rare in the promotion sweepstakes. The easier the job and the more congenial the situation, the less attractive the job is likely to be in the promotion context.[4] Recall the guidance received from football coaches: always push against the block because your adversary is always trying to push you away from the play. The worst career advice you can receive is to "go with the flow."

Overseas Tours

You will find a greater proportion of overseas billets than there used to be, and they are in more challenging locales. The odds are high that you will be ordered overseas at some point in your career. Today's detailers and their bosses recognize the challenges associated with overseas tours and look favorably on the records of officers who have accepted the assignment, especially those who agree to overseas *sea* duty, not spending three to four years in London. One detailer notes:

> The longer an officer sticks around, the more likely it is that he or she will get that phone call or e-mail telling him or her it is time to pay the piper. In general the more senior one gets, the tougher it becomes to pack up and move to Japan, Italy, Guam, or Korea. The best advice is to volunteer to go when it is in your best professional and personal interest to do so. It is easier to knock out an overseas tour (1) when single; (2) while married before kids; (3) while married with school-age kids but before the health of one's parents or in-laws becomes a concern.[5]

Look forward to your rotation orders as another opportunity to broaden your career background. How you should perform to get the orders you want is discussed later in the book when we consider your relationship with detailers and placement officers.

10

Command and Staff Assignments
Fast Tracks and Dead Ends

My best advice is to march to the sound of guns.
—Anonymous

A captain can do no wrong if he but lays his ship alongside one of
the enemy.
—Lord Nelson

This chapter is for officers who want to make their careers in the Navy unrestricted line. In short, they want to become skippers of ships, aviation squadrons, or seagoing special warfare units. Readers who aspire to promotion in the supply corps, civil engineering corps, or the various other staff and restricted-line specialties can skip this chapter.

For the rest of you gathered around, you have probably already figured out that command and preparing yourself for it is the name of the game. Only the rare bird in the unrestricted line makes captain in the Navy without having had a command tour, preferably at sea and preferably a successful one. For most unrestricted-line aspirants, their first command tour occurs in the grade of commander. A few pass that milestone earlier in their career, but almost all have to achieve command in the grade of commander to stay in the professional performance and promotion success business.

Although all services place great emphasis on command experience, for the naval officer it is the only game in town, the star we steer by. No officers are considered proven until they have served in command. No responsibility is so absolute as command at sea. All the good staff jobs in the world, no matter how ably performed, cannot rescue a resume that does not have a successful command tour. The Navy ethos places shore duty and staff duty much further down the line in importance. They are necessary but not central to the Navy's mission. Somebody must perform those duties, and there are benefits, for example, improving your understanding of the Navy as a whole, broadening your service reputation among other warfare specialties, and providing an opportunity for more home life. Just as Horatio Alger wrote, "Go west, young man!" a sea daddy will tell you, "Go to sea, young man (or woman), and prepare yourself for command."

Why is there this seemingly myopic focus on sea duty and command? It is what the Navy is all about, where the forces are, where the action is, and where the challenges of battle with the enemy are faced and met. It is where you put your career on the line every day. It is where Sailors are an integral part of your life and a leadership challenge. This saliency of command is a fact of life of the sea service and always has been. Its roots go back to the early days of the Navy when the shore establishment was nearly nonexistent. If you were a naval officer, you were at sea, or you were ashore on half pay. By definition a naval officer was a sea officer. Of course, the Navy has changed, and we now have a massive shore establishment to support a highly complex and technical Navy. And there are many command billets ashore—in the training establishment, recruiting offices, fleet support activities, and industrial support base of the service. But nothing beats the visibility, prestige, and professional growth opportunity of a sea command billet.

In his landmark work, *The Naval Profession*, Vice Adm. James Calvert describes the mark that command experience stamps on a naval officer:

> Leaving aside the personal satisfactions of command, there are some longer term rewards. Successful ship command almost always leaves a man different for having had it. To those who have not witnessed the change in

others, the statement probably sounds pompous and conceited. But again and again, I have seen young men I have known for a long time take their first command and with it responsibilities and authority they have not known before. In the two or three years that they hold that command, if they hold it successfully—and the great majority do—a definite change in self-confidence, decisiveness, and self-reliance comes about. For those who may think the effects of command at sea are all on the overbearing side, let me hasten to add that if there is a single man who has not learned humility during his tour in command, then he has either escaped the usual experiences or he is impervious to such instruction. In short, command at sea is a great teacher, and fortunate is the man who stays with the naval profession long enough to go through this course of instruction. He will benefit from it all his life, regardless of what he may later do.[1]

There are pecking orders in the pyramid of command desirability. At the top are the combatant commands—combat ships, aviation squadrons, and various deploying embarked units. Next are the deploying logistic units, units that are necessary to sustain and support the combatant units. Next are various shore-based fleet support units. Finally, there is the shore establishment itself. Make no mistake: all these categories are necessary for a combat-ready Navy. Nevertheless, some commands are more desirable than others if we judge on the basis of the success of their skippers before promotion boards. And, not surprisingly, the top flag billets in the Navy (four-star officers) are reserved for officers of the unrestricted line, those who have proved themselves at sea.

Within each category there is also a pecking order. Surface warfare officers aspire to command of destroyers and cruisers (although amphibs are slowly catching up in popularity), naval aviation officers aspire to command of carrier squadrons and eventually air wings or carriers, and submarine officers aspire to command of submarines. Smaller subcommunities, such as patrol aviation, mine forces, and special warfare, have their own pecking orders.

If a successful command tour and multiple preparatory sea tours are so important, two questions arise. What is the pathway to command? How do officers prepare themselves for such a race? Let me suggest that it starts very early in one's career. Although initial missteps can be overcome, it becomes more difficult to correct for wrong turns or less than excellent performance as tour builds on tour. View your career as building a brick wall, laying one brick on another. Poor foundations lead to less than optimal careers. I will have more to say about this subject later in the book when I advise midshipmen and officer candidates. At this point my advice is: go to sea early and often, select combatant forces as your focus, do your utmost to perform well to make your command and skipper successful, and prepare yourself meticulously for your boss's job.

Staff duty along the way will broaden your professional perspective and expose you to the notice and leadership of some of the Navy's top people. But staff duty cannot be the strength of your resume if you aspire to command. In the other services you might make a career of staff duty, but not so in the Navy. Staffs are a way station, not a destination for the ambitious naval officer. You will be advised along the way to add to your formal education at the war colleges or at postgraduate education institutions. And if you aspire to flag rank, you must attend a professional military education program at some point. But for now, consider further formal education opportunities very carefully. Large doses are a career killer—tragic but true.

With regard to staff duty, staffs are necessary as long as we have large organizations. Admirals are necessary at sea as long as naval forces include many (often differing) units that must act in concert. Staffs help the admiral plan, decide, and supervise. Staff officers are not in charge of anything outside the confines of the staff. Their role is to gather information, plan, advise, and monitor. They do not act for the admiral except in areas where the admiral's policy and intent are very clear. They are not in command. And they do not bear ultimate responsibility for the performance of the units under their admiral's command. Their role, although very important, reminds me of the old observation that staff officers are like altered tomcats: they still go out at night—but only in an advisory capacity.

With the exceptions noted below, consider staff duties an adjunct to your career, not the main route. The biggest exception is, of course, duty on a staff in Washington. Almost all Washington duty is staff duty, but there it is staff duty of a special kind. The closer to the top you are, the closer you are to determining (or seeing determined) the future of your service. The further away from the top you are (for example, a destroyer squadron staff or an air wing commander's staff), the more you see how today's Navy operates. But if you are alert, you can learn about today's operations in your ship and squadron tours and move on to having your staff duty in Washington, where to a large degree the Navy's and your future will be determined.

II

Washington Duty

> Once you leave the tactical and operational level the key decisions
> that affect your service's and the nation's future are made in
> Washington. To avoid duty there is in neither the nation's nor your
> best interest.
>
> —Counsel from a senior flag officer

As a junior officer you are not yet thinking about Washington duty. It is
more likely that your first shore duty will be in one of the service's schoolhouses. But by your second shore tour, the odds of your going to Washington
duty are very high. To come ashore from a challenging sea billet to an office
in the Washington bureaucracy where the office's product is not at all
apparent—or, if apparent, seemingly unimportant—can be a real letdown.
Yet if you are not at sea, your career is usually best served by duty in
Washington (or headquarters that are an extension of Washington, such as
the Naval Personnel Command in Millington, Tennessee, or the Naval Air
Systems Command at Patuxent River, Maryland).[1]

The more senior you get, the more time you will and should spend in
Washington because that is where the major decisions that employ today's
Navy and create tomorrow's Navy are made. If you are interested in a top
Navy job someday, you have to understand how those decisions are made
and in your own modest way contribute to them. It will not be fun; the
hours are often long, and, unfortunately, the shorter they are, the more
likely you reside in a career backwater.

A few flag officers take pride in the fact that they never had Washington duty. For the most part they belong to a different era, or they will have a difficult time getting in the running for the Navy's top jobs. Unfortunately, being a "good operator" (a high accolade) is not enough. You also need to be a good force acquisition, management, planning, or budgeting person or some combination of these. And you learn that in Washington. One of the more disturbing sights in Washington is to run into flag officers who are on their first Washington assignment. They are learning in a hurry and are probably too late. They pine to get back to sea, but they will likely never again get there while on active duty. What does Washington duty do for your promotion prospects? There are many answers to this question

Washington: Where the Top Jobs Are

Most of the Navy's flag (and even captain) jobs are in the Washington area or associated headquarters. If you aspire to high rank, you must spend most of your time ashore as a senior officer in Washington. Washington tours are also the precondition for getting the top jobs in the fleet. How does this work?

By the time you are a senior commander or captain, you have had or are in your second or subsequent Washington tour. You are learning how the Navy plans for its future, budgets and programs to survive in the funding world, prospers in the joint world, and supports the operations of the fleet at the major headquarters level. You are learning the trade of getting things done in the nation's capital. It is rather like watching sausage being made. It is not pretty, but unfortunately it is necessary. These preparatory tours are important for your career. You should be looking ahead to the day when your promotion jacket is before the flag selection board and its members are asking each other the following: What can this officer do to help us carry the Navy's load at headquarters as well as at sea? They ask this question because your first billet after you are selected for flag rank probably will be in Washington. As a junior flag officer in Washington, you will be doing important Navy business—and looking to get to a flag job afloat. You will not get that afloat job if you do not perform well in Washington, and you cannot expect to perform well in Washington as a boot flag officer if it is your first tour there. It is that simple.

Getting Known

A senior of mine, a war hero and unfortunately not destined to make flag, once remarked to me, "The biggest mistake I made in my career was not to get known." What he meant was that although he had a good record—and in combat at that—he never looked for assignments that broadened his resume. He had only one brief Washington tour and was always in a lather to get back to the fleet. His desire was understandable, except that it did little to expand the basis for his service reputation beyond his warfare community.

For most of us our Washington tours are our first extended and close-up experience interacting with officers in other warfare specialties. If you are a ship driver, you have had little opportunity for such interaction with aviators and submariners. And the same applies to officers who serve in those specialties. In Washington the odds are high that you will be working for an officer in another warfare specialty and that your daily business will be conducted with officers outside your warfare community. This is an important opportunity to lay your professional competence before a larger audience. Although your future screening boards will be comprised of seniors from your warfare community, they will be in a minority in your future promotion boards.

In observing selection boards over the years, many senior officers have come to the conclusion that it is often officers from other communities whose vote pushes you over the top into the promised land of promotion. It is not enough for your community to be high on you; your record must persuade others, too. The spadework to get their vote usually starts with your Washington assignments with a set of fitness reports signed by bosses outside your warfare specialty but well known by board members from those communities.

Networking

It is the rare officer on duty in Washington who does not have to work with departments and commands outside his own. Much of the work in Washington involves working with other offices. This need results in a great deal of networking to get the Navy's business done. A by-product is that you get known outside of your own office and get a reputation as a doer or a roadblock, a person who works the problem or one who bucks it up to his boss, someone who is a team player or a loner. There is another important by-product, too: when you get back to the fleet, you will know how Washington works. You will not be intimidated by the bureaucracy (you were once part of it), and you will not hesitate for long to call a contact in Washington to get the answers or support you need.

A Word about Washington Working Hours

Some of you may be looking forward to your Washington tour, thinking you may have an opportunity to spend more time with your family after back-to-back arduous overseas deployments. Think again. Unfortunately, the more regular and more predictable your working hours in Washington, the further away you are from the real action. I do not mean to say here that long working hours should be your objective. True, some offices work long hours because that is the boss's style, and some even enjoy it for the bragging rights it brings. But in most offices, long working hours mean that things are happening or about to happen and that the organization is responding or trying to get out ahead of the problem. A phone call from a congressional staffer on needed funding or a bill before the committee stimulates the system. So does that late phone call (inevitably on a Friday afternoon when you are cleaning out your in-basket) from an official in the office of the secretary of defense or from a four-star fleet commander. Your chain of command may be so busy putting out fires during regular working hours that they find that the routine work in the in-basket must be done after most of the other offices are closing down.

The point of this discussion is that when you hear a shop has working hours that run from eight in the morning to five in the afternoon, be wary and skeptical about assignment there. Chances are that they are not close to the heartbeat of the action or that the product of that shop is routine staffing. As a corollary look carefully at the shop that is working long hours so you can satisfy yourself that their work is really all that important and that their bosses carry a lot of weight in the larger scheme of things. I will not give you a list here of offices in Washington that are central to Navy decision making. The list changes from time to time. But put your ear to the ground and find out what is really going on.

Follow the Dollars

The power in Washington resides closest to the dollars, that is, getting them from the Congress and spending them on the things the Navy most needs. One officer famously remarked: "If you don't control the dollars, you don't have a program." Many naval officers coming to Washington want to get close to the heartbeat of their warfare specialty. Fresh from the fleet, they want to work with such things as weapons requirements and programming. After all, they know something about what is needed and how it will be used. But there is another reason as well. Offices close to their warfare specialty are where the people are who will most help them before screening and promotion boards. So assignment to those offices tends to be personally satisfying and career enhancing.

Nevertheless, do not overlook the shops that control the dollars for those systems you are most keen on getting into the fleet or better maintaining those that are already there. Most crunches in Washington are dollar related, just as most problems in your household are likely to be. Get close to the dollars, and you will get close to making things happen. I have in mind the comptroller and budget shops that are spread throughout the

Washington headquarters scene. Detailers underline the point that the Navy does place great emphasis on money-related billets, and they cite telling evidence from their tours as recorders for command screening boards. "Wait a minute!" you say. "I didn't enter the Navy to be an accountant!" That is true, but your Navy is not going anywhere without the dollars to pay the bills, including your paycheck.

The Importance of the Job Title

Some people argue that the title of the job makes the person, but this is not true. I knew a senior commander who was offered a job in Washington that was normally filled by a senior captain. He was to be the deputy to a flag officer in a shop that was central to the planning of a major bureau (now a field command). As it turned out, he had no choice—he had to go. Shortly after he took the job, the billet was downgraded from a deputy to the big man to "an assistant to . . ." He was put in charge of a dog's breakfast of special programs instead of standing at the boss's elbow while he made the big decisions. It turned out well because several of those programs became very big ones. He had his hands full—and before it was over he wished he had been a senior captain so as to have the clout to do the programs justice.

The lesson is: listen carefully when a detailer sells a billet on the basis of a grand-sounding title or on the basis that the job calls for an officer in the next senior grade. Likewise, beware of words that you were hand-picked for the job or faced tough competition to become the favored one.

Faded Glories

There was a time within the memory of living Navy retirees when the places to be in Washington were the Bureau of Navigation (later the Bureau of Personnel), the Strategic Planning Division of the CNO's staff, and the Bureau of Ordnance (for surface officers) or the Bureau of Aeronautics (for aviators). Many, if not most, of the officers who had senior positions in these shops eventually got at least three stars, and a disproportionate number went on to four stars. Successors of these offices still exist in Washington or in associated headquarters farther afield. They all still need good officers, but they are no longer the glory holes and plum assignments they once were. They get their share of promotions and flag selectees, but fashions change.

Looking closer at hand today, you will find that some offices are becoming the province of specialists in the unrestricted line or of officers in the restricted line or staff corps. For example, piece by piece, line officers are getting out of the logistics business (N4) as the specialists take over. Similar things are happening in the C⁴I (N6) and the intelligence (N2) businesses. As a line officer you will be competing with officers who have made a career of the specialty you are trying to learn. Detailers are sensitive to this shift, but they have billets to fill, and you could become a sacrificial lamb. There are advantages to you and the Navy in finding yourself a line officer among specialists, but they are seldom obvious at fitness report time.

The flag-maker billets are now more in the following areas: executive assistants to any four-star officer in Washington (and to a lesser extent elsewhere) and what I call the major secretaries and their undersecretaries (Department of Defense, Navy); key captain jobs in the warfare specialty shops (surface, sub, air); key (and successful) program managers in the systems commands; and those who run the Navy's finances (what have been called the "dollar shops"). Some have ridden White House and joint duty as their primary vehicles to flag rank. Fleet maintainers, logisticians, and personnel program managers have been somewhat less fortunate (compared to former times). But the really outstanding performers in those less-visible slots get widely known in Washington and in the fleet and will not be denied their flag.

Family Life and Social Life

Officers coming to Washington for their first tour are surprised at the change in the social scene compared to their last command. Most offices have little social life except for an occasional "hail and farewell." Departing colleagues are usually honored at a lunch, if at all. Nevertheless, there are some social opportunities that are both fun and a help in getting known. These are the various festivities sponsored by the separate warfare communities, the annual Navy Relief Ball, class reunions for Naval Academy graduates at nearby Annapolis, and gatherings by graduates of civilian universities that have a Washington alumni chapter. Unfortunately, the Pentagon community resides in the District of Columbia and into the far reaches of Virginia and Maryland (some commute from as far away as West Virginia), so opportunities for a service-oriented social life are more limited than you enjoyed in the fleet. But in my experience it is well worthwhile from both a personal enjoyment and a professional advancement standpoint to keep up your social connections and get a change of pace from the office atmosphere.

An advantage of Washington duty often overlooked is that your neighbors, fellow churchgoers, PTA members, and den mothers will likely be civilians. Although they may have government jobs, they know little about the services. You will find this interaction a broadening experience—and more accessible than in the more service-oriented communities where you last served.

12

Career Tracks for the Unrestricted Line

> There is something conceptual, almost mathematically pure about
> life at sea—and at the same time hard and real which engages one
> more deeply and demands greater responsibility than is needed
> on land.
>
> —Goran Schildt, *In the Wake of the Witch*

Naval officers follow four obligatory stops on the road to promotion in the
unrestricted line: (1) one or more sea tours as a junior officer, (2) a sea tour
as a department head of a ship or squadron, (3) a command at sea, usually in the grade of commander, and (4) a major command at sea or ashore
while serving in the grade of captain. The first sea tour may be split with
two ship tours or consist of a single extended ship or squadron tour. During
these early tours officers learn the trade of going to sea, flying, or both. They
typically serve as junior division officers and division officers. The surface
warfare officers win basic warfare qualifications as an officer of the deck or
other watch officer afloat. They earn the surface warfare pin and start the
journey to qualification as a department head. Submarine officers have
much the same path but must also qualify as a chief engineer in submarines.
Aviation junior officers qualify in all aspects of flying their aircraft, including various types of weapons delivery. Patrol plane aviators qualify for the
coveted patrol plane commander (PPC) designation.

The second major sea tour occurs in the grade of senior lieutenant or lieutenant commander. Surface warfare officers attend the department head course at the Surface Warfare Officers School (SWOS). The object of this sea tour is to qualify for and serve a meaningful tour as a department head afloat, including an overseas deployment if possible. During this tour the sorting out for eventual command occurs. Competition among officers serving in their department head tours is intense, and rankings for recommendations for promotion are critical to screening for command in a later sea tour. Some officers serve as executive officer in this or the next sea tour. The executive officer tour is a prerequisite for assignment to command.[1]

Assignment to the third sea tour, command in the grade of commander, is critical to your future. In that command, you are competing with your fellow skippers, who have survived as tough a screening process as you have. You will likely need a successful sea command tour in the grade of commander to be promoted to captain. Some make it to captain without it, but they have very specialized qualifications and are rare birds indeed.

The fourth or fifth sea tour is usually the major command tour either at sea or ashore. The sea commands include amphibious, destroyer, and submarine squadrons; aircraft carriers and air wings; cruisers; and major amphibious and service force ships or squadrons.[2] Moreover, because there are important commands ashore that need quality skippers, some of the best officers qualifying for major command fill them. These commands include the major naval stations (e.g., Norfolk and San Diego), naval air stations (e.g., Oceana and North Island), and some of the major schoolhouses. A major command is the capstone of an officer's career. Only the best captains are selected to fill them, and they compose the pool from which the next flag officers are picked. The competition is fierce. The best and not so good quickly become apparent not only to their seniors but also to their peers.

At each step of this progression of sea duty from junior officer afloat to major command afloat, a premium is placed on serving during an overseas deployment. Better yet is a deployment that involves contingency or combat operations. You want to be tested and found able, and selection boards place great store on superior service in tough circumstances. Not everyone is fortunate enough to get a deployment or a contingency operation or see combat on their sea tours, and selection and screening boards realize that. For example, in the 1991 Gulf War about half of the Navy's combatant ships and squadrons saw service in that theater. It was just the luck of the rotation draw for an officer to serve in the Persian Gulf during that time. Moreover, many officers were serving ashore in the United States during that war. If you did not see active service during the Gulf War, it was not a mark against you, but if you did so serve and do well, it was a plus on your record. Similar comments apply to the 2001–4 wars in the Middle East.

The entire subject of serving in overseas deployments, participating in contingencies, and seeing combat (and doing well) is one of the few aspects of a naval career that is heavily dependent on the luck of the draw or good timing. To some degree your future is decided by the conduct of the nation's adversaries. That said, you should actively seek assignment to a unit that is or will be deployed during your tours afloat. In some cases, this may mean back-to-back deployments at some cost to a decent family life.

If you are less fortunate or for some personal reason you seek such assignment, you might arrive on board a ship just going into the yard for an extended overhaul or modification. Or you might be detached just before a major overseas deployment after surviving the crucible of the predeployment work-up. Depending on your unit's rotation cycle, you will find the next unluckiest timing to be joining your ship or squadron the day it returns from deployment. But some would argue that such timing gets you in on the ground floor in preparing for the next deployment. One popular preference is to join a deployer midway in the work-up cycle. That course, however, requires that you hit the deck running because your ship or squadron is usually in high-tempo training operations, and you will have some catching up to do.

The First Shore Tour

Between the obligatory sea tours described above, there are the just-as-obligatory shore tours. Here I cannot offer a one-size-fits-all suggestion on how to manage your career. For aviators the first shore tour will probably involve instructor duty in the training command, replacement squadron (RAG), or other flying billet. It might involve a tour at the Naval Postgraduate School. A fortunate and able few may be assigned to test-pilot school or the Blue Angels. Surface and submarine offices on their first shore tour might be involved in a schoolhouse tour either as a student or an instructor (e.g., SWOS, Naval Academy, Naval Postgraduate School, Chief of Naval Education and Training [CNET] staff). A few junior officers on their first tour ashore might find themselves in Washington.

The Second Shore Tour

The second shore tour is very important. Many will be in the Washington headquarters area or in such major outlying hubs as Pensacola, Millington, San Diego, or Norfolk. A tour as a relatively junior officer in Washington is of immense help in preparing you for later and critically important Washington tours in your career. During this tour you will learn the basics of the Washington game. Still, you do not want just any Washington tour. You should strive for assignment to an important shop and one with a history of being led by the Navy's brightest officers. Working hours from eight in the morning to five in the afternoon and handling office routine are not for you if you want to see how the important parts of the Navy really work and be a part of it.

A War College Tour

At some point just before or just after your third shore tour, you may be ordered to attend one of the service war colleges. If you aspire to very high rank, a PME tour at one of the war colleges is a must. One crusty former commanding officer stated, "Commander command is the last screening board that focuses primarily on your operational record. After that the Navy is looking at everything else that you bring to the table."[3] As important as the PME ticket is, keep your attention on your goal. You must screen for that commander command to progress, and your tour sequence to get there is your most important near-term objective. If you feel crowded at this point, with too much to do and not enough time to do it, you are in good company!

The Third Shore Tour

At this point you are serving as a senior commander or a newly selected captain and should be in one of the Washington area headquarters.[4] There is at least one exception to this general rule: assignment to a joint or combined command headquarters overseas or in Norfolk or Hawaii. At some point you should get your joint assignment, and this tour may be it. You will have another opportunity on your next shore tour, but you are getting fairly senior by that point, and you may get a better career-enhancing offer that does not involve joint duty. A look down the road shows that it helps to go before the flag board with your joint tour already completed.

Later Shore Tours

Junior readers may skip the discussion about later shore tours unless they are curious about what may lie a decade or two downstream. You senior readers may find yourselves in Washington after having successfully completed your major command tour. Many believe that, to be really in the flag race, you must—in addition to having had a major command—have also served in a very demanding shore or sea staff billet. These billets include (but are not limited to): key post–major command billets on the staffs of the Chief of Naval Operations, the Naval Personnel Command, and the Systems Commands; key billets in the Joint Staff of the Joint Chiefs of Staff; Commandant of Midshipmen at the Naval Academy; Chiefs of Staff to the Commanders of the Numbered Fleets; executive assistants to any four-star officer of any service; and any flag billet being filled with a captain for an extended period.

Billets that do not qualify under this criterion (but probably should) are chief of staff to type commanders and destroyer, submarine, carrier, and amphibious groups; most schoolhouse command billets; most captain billets in the recruiting command; and most captain jobs overseas. Of course, as in any such listing, there are exceptions, but the odds of making flag get even longer when your comparative performance or assignment preferences place you in billets outside the mainstream. Those who make flag after an unconventional career are the subject of much attention within the service. Most officers admire the pluck of those who survived the rigors of paths less traveled and came out near the top of their profession.

Flag Shore Tours

If you are a newly minted flag officer, you probably were selected on your current shore tour or while serving in your major command. You are most likely in Washington or soon will be. Now you are benefiting from previous tours in or near the nation's capital or in outlying headquarters. This is an apprentice flag tour for you, and you are already looking to return to sea for an all-too-brief stint as a group commander afloat with your own personal flag flying from the truck.

You already know that now is no time to rest on your hard-earned laurels. The competition for the few one- and two-star flag sea billets is intense. Only the best serving in the most demanding jobs get the nod. The race for promotion to two-star rank is already well under way, and many will not make it. At this point the CNO, assisted by the vice chief of naval operations (VCNO) and the chief of naval personnel, is your detailer. The process is called "slating" and involves fitting several hundred pieces into several hundred slots. Your personal preferences carry little weight. You go where you are needed. The high card you hold in all this is your performance record. The CNO simply cannot afford to put the best flag officers in lesser (though still important) billets. Moreover, all flag nominations that result from slating must be cleared with the secretary of the Navy. With few exceptions, however, the secretary is concerned mostly with three-star and above nominations that must go to the secretary of defense and the White House and thence to the Senate for approval and confirmation.

If you are disappointed and get what you consider is a less-than-the-best billet, you should bear up and recall the advice of one senior flag officer: "There are no bad flag billets!" He cited cases of future three- and four-star officers who served well in junior and somewhat obscure billets before moving on to better things. That said, there remains the possibility that you may not get past the two-star selection board and that you will have your three or four years in Washington or ashore elsewhere and then head home to pasture. You will have run a good race, but a second, third, or fourth star is not in your future.

But if you do get the brass ring and get one of the coveted flag sea billets, chances are that you will only serve there for a year or so before you will be ordered back to Washington. You are no longer a boot flag officer, and you are on your way to two stars or already have them. Now you are put into a demanding flag billet where you are in the ring fighting for the Navy's dollar and forces. You are one of the warfare barons on the CNO's staff (surface, sub, air), a budgeteer or program director, or a vice commander of one of the system commands. You are one of the wheels that will make things happen for good or ill in the Navy now and in the future.

The CNO and VCNO know you and call you by your first name—and they depend mightily on you. Welcome to the three-star race.[5]

The hot-running two stars in Washington (and a few in the hinterland or overseas) compose the crop from which the three-star officers are picked. The best or those with the most potential head to the numbered fleets. Others head for type commander or other three-star shore slots. For those going to the numbered fleets, another Washington tour is in their future. For those going to other three-star jobs, their next port will probably be the farm. Only the best get two three-star tours back-to-back.[6]

As a three-star officer returning to Washington, you are a contestant in the four-star race. The qualifications for four-star rank are very rigorous, and again some luck enters the equation. By this point, some officers have health problems and regrettably must retire. Some incumbent four-star officers similarly fall by the wayside and must be relieved unexpectedly. Some four-star billets require special qualifications in joint or combined staff experience. Most have to be acceptable to the other service chiefs as well as to the CNO. All have to be approved by the secretary of defense. It is a tough race for all these billets, and each service puts its best candidates forward. To have earned a reputation as an effective team player in Washington and in the joint arena are real pluses. In a few cases the four-star assignment (the stars go with the job) is a reward for a difficult job well done. For others it is more a matter of seniority. Many four stars have other four stars working for them as component commanders, and ideally the boss should be senior by time in grade. The rules are fluid but in most instances come back to performance and service reputation—where we started this book.

What are the lessons for the junior officer in this distant promised land of flag promotions, assignments, and eventual retirement? First, do not take it too seriously. You have much work to do—and fun to experience—before you need to think about what admirals do and how they get there. Second, a naval career is a long journey, and being successful requires stamina and a problem-solving mind-set. Third, Sailor or aviator skills are important in the earlier years of a career. As you get more senior, however, leading, managing, planning, motivating, innovating, and integrating become the most important talents. Savvy junior officers see life and their career as a continuum of change. There is life after a career of flying and ship driving is over. Enjoy it now, but recognize that eventually the enterprise will require that you grow to lead it—not just fly it or sail it.

Midshipmen being instructed in military etiquette during the first days of their naval service. Knowledge of etiquette, both military and social, is an essential part of an officer's professional tool kit from the first day of service and on into eventual retirement. *U.S. Navy photo by PH2 Damon J. Moritz*

Midshipmen coming and going. The photo above shows a plebe class at the Naval Academy being sworn in, and the one on the next page shows a senior class taking its commissioning oath. Both oaths are a promise of faithful service and an implicit willingness to accept responsibility for results, not just good intentions. *U.S. Naval Academy photo*

U.S. Naval Academy photo by Robert de Gast

A representative of the Navy Personnel Command answers questions on career management during a briefing to officers stationed in Sasebo, Japan. Although Navy personnel authorities conduct numerous briefings, symposia, and field trips to answer questions about career management, it is up to the individual to keep up to date on the subject and to perform at a high level that leads to good assignments and promotions. *U.S. Navy photo by PHAN Ian W. Anderson*

Good service and good deeds follow Sailors into their retirement. Shown is a group of Norfolk, Virginia, veterans unveiling *The Homecoming* statue honoring the Navy family. *U.S. Navy photo by Martin Maddock*

A rare photograph of seven former chiefs of naval operations. Adm. Arleigh Burke (*far right*) and Adm. Thomas Moorer (*second from right*) were the towering naval figures of their eras and were marked for high office early in their careers. *U.S. Navy photo by PH1 Paul J. Salesi*

Good performance leads to good assignments, and good performance in those assignments leads to promotions. Above, an executive officer (*right*) relieves his commanding officer aboard USS *Saipan* (LHA 2). *U.S. Navy photo by PH2 Robert M. Schalk*

A junior officer briefing his Visit, Board, Search, and Seizure Team aboard USS *O'Bannion* (DD 987). The ability to speak effectively and decisively with subordinates is a key career skill, one that can be learned with practice. *U.S. Navy photo by PH1 Marthaellen L. Ball*

A major command is the capstone of any officer's career. This is a change of command aboard USS *Carl Vinson* (CVN 70). *U.S. Navy photo by PHAN C. Solseth*

Family support is a key component of officer effectiveness, and an effective officer leads to an effective ship or squadron. Shown here is the homecoming for the executive officer of USS *Toledo* (SSN 769). *U.S. Navy photo by Ethan Macnow*

There is no high in life to compare with the return to homeport after an arduous cruise. Here, an officer from USS *Constellation* (CV 64) responds to questions from a television reporter while holding his daughter, whom he is seeing for the first time. *U.S. Navy photo by PH2 Elizabeth J. Lewis*

Above, Adm. Ernest J. King shares a joke with friends. Below, a more familiar portrait of King as a tough, often ruthless, and effective officer who led the United States Navy to victory in World War II. *U.S. Navy photos*

As officers rise in rank and serve in positions of responsibility, their ability to deal effectively and courteously with senior officials and representatives of foreign governments assumes even greater importance. Above, the commanding officer of USS *Vandegrift* (FFG 48) greets Russian naval visitors on his ship. *U.S. Navy photo by PH2 Robert S. Cole*

Screening and promotion selection boards are the key gateways to good assignments and promotions. They have a tough task, and few officers challenge their basic fairness. *U.S. Navy photo by JO2 Jeff Nichols*

This midshipman is reaching high early in her naval career. She is selecting her first ship during service assignment night at the Naval Academy. Service selection is a key milestone in a naval career and has major repercussions in setting the boundaries and opportunities in an officer's professional journey. *U.S. Naval Academy photo by Wayne McCleg*

13

Promotion to Flag Rank

Admirals still die on the bridges of their flagships
while generals die in bed.
—Attributed to Gen. Merrill B. Twining

For junior officers who have traveled this far, any discussion of flag promotions must seem unreal. You just got here, and already I am talking about the end of a career! Moreover, most of you entered the Navy for reasons other than promotions. You are to be congratulated for your motivations, but now that you are here, you cannot help looking around you and saying: "Why not me?" Or perhaps you have been in long enough to say, "If I were the admiral (or the CNO), I would correct this or that." Again, congratulations! You see rank and promotions as a way to get good things done. The longer you stay in, the more the prospect of promotion will appeal you. You should pause occasionally and take the long view of your career—but as I said in closing the last chapter, do not overdo it.

I need to say up front that many officers have little interest in promotion to flag even when they are well launched on their naval careers. Others looking into their mirrors confess to themselves that they are not cut out for the job. Moreover, the sacrifices needed to stay in the race are not all that attractive to them. Others, and perhaps a majority, are so enamored of the mechanics and the here and now of the profession—ship handling, flying, leading enlisted personnel, going to sea, visiting foreign ports, the adventure of change in duty station, and so on—that they have little time to consider promotion except when the lack thereof means shortening a personally rewarding career. For them promotion to the rank of captain seems the pinnacle of their naval service. The simple arithmetic of the promotion pyramid means we need officers like those just described. They do the heavy lifting on the deck plates, in the hangars, and the other day-to-day work of making the Navy function. There is nothing wrong with not aspiring to flag rank—or to captain, for that matter. In the last chapter of this book we will examine the importance of knowing yourself and your capabilities, interests, and limitations. But here we look at how the Navy selects its top leadership.

Most of the captains I have encountered over a full career were fully qualified for flag rank. I consider these able captains, particularly those who had held a major command, to be the real backbone of the naval service. The fact that they did not make flag rank was a matter of numbers, not qualifications. As a captain about to retire, you may look back on a productive, honorable, and even glorious career. When you return to civilian life, it is enough that you served honorably as a captain in the Navy to warrant the respect and admiration of your new neighbors, old friends, and former shipmates.

For those still left in the race for flag, the hard work and dedicated service continue. The competition is very keen; roughly only one in ten captains will be selected for flag rank. Other than the competition and the odds, what makes promotion to flag rank different? What is the flag board looking for that is so different from consideration for promotion to the more junior ranks?

Perhaps the biggest difference is that there are relatively few flag billets—measured in the several hundreds rather than thousands of captain's billets. Thus the flag board in selecting has a very precise idea of the needs of the service. If there is any doubt on that score, the flag board receives specific guidance from the convening authority, the secretary of the Navy, and information from the chief of naval personnel on the billets to be filled. Although all selection boards attempt to gauge the probable future performance of the officers being considered, the flag board takes this task even more seriously than the others. They are selecting the members of the board of directors of the Navy, officers who will lead the Navy at sea and ashore, officers who will put in place the systems and personnel with which the Navy will fight over several future decades, perhaps as long as a half century.

Something else different about the selection of flag officers is that the officers selected must demonstrate a different type of leadership. To this point officers under consideration have commanded individual ships, squadrons, and relatively small tactical formations below battle group in size. But those selected for flag will command battle groups, battle forces, and eventually battle fleets. Some of them will have major responsibilities in the shore establishment and control billions of dollars and thousands of personnel. They must command or manage through multiple echelons, not a few departments and a somewhat larger number of divisions. They must show promise of being able to develop policies and manage operations that flow through many others while setting the tone for the whole. In addition, they must be able to work effectively with other offices in and outside the Department of Defense. As flag officers the scope of their duties will expand both horizontally and vertically.

Most of the time the board picks good operators. The officers are good ship handlers, "good sticks" (the aviation expression), good with Sailors, and good at keeping their bosses happy. Even with these qualifications, though, some will not measure up to the level of skill needed to manage and lead truly large enterprises. Their valuable expertise is largely limited to the unit level. With this danger in mind, the flag selection board must extrapolate from the records before them to pick those who will best handle these expanded responsibilities.[1] There is an important point to be reiterated here. A fitness report jacket is a log of past accomplishments and shortcomings and is not by itself a predictor of the future. Thus the flag board is less interested in how good a ship handler you were (they expect you to have that skill) than in the even better decision maker you may become. They are looking for clues in your jacket as to your potential to grow into very demanding duties and responsibilities.

You might respond: "Is that not what all promotion boards are looking for?" The answer is yes. But flag boards are different because they are picking the people who will lead and command the whole enterprise called the United States Navy. Mistakes made by lesser boards can inflict damage on the institution, but bad flag picks strike the institution at its foundations. So, this is serious business.

Specific Characteristics Required

What specifically is the flag board looking for? The short answer is: a group of relatively young leaders who will help the current flag community pull the Navy's wagon. They are looking not for show horses, but workhorses. They want people who got things done wherever they served. They want people with supple minds, who can represent the Navy within the Department of Defense, before Congress, and to the American people— and confound our enemies. Good operational skills are a given, though occasionally the board will select a few officers with very specialized skills that outweigh any lack of sparkle in their operational resume.

Other skills are also sought. The board is looking for people who know the system and the book but also know that flag officers occasionally need to go outside the system or the book to get things done. The trick is to know when such initiatives are needed. Rockers, shakers, and movers are in. Personal empire builders and political officers are out, and smart, aggressive problem solvers are in.

Now the question to ask yourself is: What are the specifics they will be looking for in my jacket or in what others say about me? I suggest the following:

1. *A good solid grounding in the basics of the naval profession (professional competence).* The board wants to see strong performance in command,

particularly a major command afloat or ashore. They will cut through the nice words (a lot have them) in the jacket and look for solid facts and data to back up your accomplishments. Good combat performance will catch their eye, but their major concern will be to see that you perform well under the pressure of events. Do you know your stuff? Should you be trusted with a group command afloat?

2. *The intangibles of character.* Honor, courage, and commitment, to use the popular phrase. Can you be trusted to do the right thing? Have you been tested? Are you stable, persistent, and gutsy?

3. *A demonstrated potential for professional growth to fill positions of greatly increased responsibility.* Could you lead other potential selectees? Would you be comfortable and effective in a realm of greatly expanded span and depth of control?

4. *A team player.* Are you a loose cannon or one who works well with diverse constituencies? The board is not looking for Mr. or Ms. Personality, but loners and self-serving types need not apply.

5. *A suppleness of mind.* Although smarts are prized, mental agility and constructive imagination anchored in reality are even more valuable. A variant of this trait is situational awareness, *an ability to see the forest and the trees at the same time* and devise a path through them that confronts or circumvents obstacles, each at the appropriate time.

6. *Needs of the service.* Is it likely that you would become a detailing problem? Where would you best serve in our Navy? Have you had your joint tour yet, or will we have to send you to a joint billet first? Have you been in Washington recently? Was the job a key one?

7. *Service reputation.* The board cannot read everything about the prospective selectee, no matter how complete or well written the jacket is. How well known by reputation are you to the board? What do people outside your warfare community say about you? Have you "stovepiped" your career (i.e., stayed mostly in your warfare community, passing through a succession of billets in that specialty, to grease the skids before screening and promotion boards), or are you a broad-gauge

officer who is well known in the service and not dependent on your warfare community connections?

These seven tests are not written down in a checklist and put before the board, but you can be sure that each board member goes through a calculus that involves all or most of these factors.

The Perspective of the President of the Board

The president of the board, as well as individual members, wants to pick the best applicant to meet the needs of the service. But the president has some additional concerns. That individual must see that the board's selectees *as a group* satisfy the guidance of the convening authority. The president is, of course, limited at the outset by the number of officers who can be selected. Still, if the convening authority suggests the need for some specific specialties or emphasizes certain types of experience, the president must make an effort to see that the board's results reflect that guidance. The last thing the president wants is for the secretary of the Navy to reject the board's list of selectees or remove a selectee from it (for cause).

In addition to following the guidance, the president of the board wants to ensure that specific warfare communities are fairly treated and represented in the final list. The president is constantly aware that only the best must be selected but knows fairness is an important factor if the Navy is to retain top flight officers in *all* communities. The results of the board will be scrutinized closely by every captain and by most others in the service. Did the selectees have a successful major command, a demanding Washington job? Which subcategories in the warfare communities fared best (e.g., air wing commanders versus carrier skippers, cruiser skippers versus destroyer squadron commodores, and amphibs versus cruiser/destroyer types)? How many selectees had advanced degrees? How many were graduates of service colleges? The questions, though they move into the realm of seemingly trivial distinctions, are ones of keen interest to one or more professional communities.

In a sense the flag board results indicate the seriousness of the Navy's leadership by its fairness in considering for promotion officers with differing professional backgrounds, their image of the future Navy, and their sense of the needs of the service. This message reverberates through the service. It exposes potential embarrassments when we do not follow our own exhortations to the service (e.g., we say the contributions of a specific community are important but then deny them proportionate representation on the promotion lists).

Now I want to say a few words about perceptions versus facts. When they are selected for flag rank, many officers are serving in executive assistant (to very senior flag officer or departmental officials) billets when the list is released. In almost all cases they have already had a successful major command tour. But often that fact is obscured by the focus on the selectee's current assignment. The impression is given that, to make flag, serving in an executive assistant billet is the key to preference. In almost all cases it is the other way around: the officer is in an executive assistant billet because of past superior performance, including in a major command billet.

Youth Versus Age

The Navy as an institution would dearly like to have the issue of youth versus age both ways. They would like the person to have the time in a career to fill all the boxes—get a postgraduate education, go to the war colleges, and get plenty of sea time *and* demanding Washington duty. They would like the officer to fit in a joint tour, have longer command tours, have more homesteading opportunities, and so on. At the same time there is pressure to promote the best earlier and hurry them to flag rank by a rapid passage through numerous qualifying billets. This pressure has been accelerated under the Defense Officer Personnel Management Act (DOPMA) and subsequent officer personnel legislation. Under current rules the vast majority of officers retire at the thirty-year point (or earlier), and only a few flag officers go on to the thirty-five-year point and beyond.[2] Rapid promotion is a key factor in the retention of the best and brightest. Therefore, it should not surprise us that some flag officers today have what in an earlier age would have been called incomplete resumes. On the plus side, they are much younger and can spend more time in the flag ranks.

Occasionally, a secretary of the Navy will become involved in this issue and caution selection boards that maturity and experience also have some value in the drive for youth and vigor. You should be aware of these cross-currents and the tradeoffs. Many believe the current balance is about right. There is room for older—and younger—flag officers, and a wise flag board is not bound by stereotypes.

In spite of the imperfections that persist in the flag selection system, it is fair by almost any standard. More work still needs to be done in seeing that smaller or less influential warfare communities receive an appropriate number of flag selections, but progress is being made. In industry, the top jobs frequently go to protégés (or relatives) of the powerful, to lateral entries as opposed to bottom-up candidates, and to those who have done very well in their most immediate past position. The naval service has few peacetime indices as concrete as the financial bottom line that characterizes the business world. The Navy's bottom line is to win. Moreover, the service demands attention to the intangibles that in business are often put aside as secondary factors (e.g., staff turnover, morale, grooming qualified successors in management, and quality of product at the margin).

What are the lessons for junior officers just starting their career? The organization is basically fair, but the training and assignment pipeline (designator and warfare platform) you enter can have a major impact on your promotion to the senior grades. The common elements on each step of the path upward are top performance in your current job, preparing to take over your boss's job in good time, and staying as close as you can to the mainstream of the naval profession—going to sea with the combat forces.

14

Awards and Decorations

The number of medals on an officer's breast varies in inverse proportion to the square of the distance of his duties from the front line.

—C. E. Montague

There was an era, which extended well into my lifetime, when the Navy gave few decorations. The Navy as an institution was very proud that its dress tunics had no adornment except the stripes of rank: few medals, no warfare or professional badges, and few service ribbons.[1] That custom started to change during the World War I, when campaign ribbons became accepted and the first warfare badges were instituted. It was not uncommon to see a senior officer with just two or three service ribbons. Few medals were awarded in that period between the world wars, and most senior officers wore no more than their stripes of rank and the Great War (World War I) victory ribbon.

After World War II and its "medal mania" there was a push within the Navy's leadership to return to the more restrained practices of the twenties and thirties. Even well into the Korean War, successive commanders of the Seventh Fleet had a very conservative awards policy. Award recommendations were downgraded or returned to the sponsoring command with a terse comment to include the citation in the officer's next fitness report. But this draconian policy did not survive long, particularly when it collided with the much more liberal policies of the other services. The Navy found that it could not turn the clock back alone.

As what was to become the extended cold war wore on, there was a new profusion of service ribbons and even more classes of medals. Joint service medals were added to parallel the services' own awards structure.[2] Most of the new Navy awards were given more for meritorious service (typically in an office) than for action in combat. The combat "V" was added to some Navy medals (e.g., the Navy Commendation Medal, the Bronze Star, and the Legion of Merit) to make it clear that the award (often awarded for noncombat performance) was for actions against the enemy.

Today awards are calibrated to every level of performance and even rank. For example, to earn the Navy Achievement Medal (NAM) one must be a junior officer or enlisted. Distinguished Service Medals are limited by common usage to senior flag officers—usually at the end of tour or on retirement. Today a Legion of Merit (LOM) might be awarded at the end of very successful tour in a major command, whereas in the past, usually just flag officers were given that award.

At one time awards and decorations were a factor in promotion because they were rare. Enlisted personnel received promotion points for certain awards. Today the number and sheer quantity of awards have resulted in a more skeptical view by screening and promotion boards. The awards are nice to have, but they are worth less than good fitness reports, though they often parallel them. Today end-of-tour awards for department heads and more senior superior performing officers are relatively common.

This award inflation has resulted in relatively junior officers and petty officers wearing two, three, or even four rows of ribbons. The perceived morale payoff for this proliferation works toward making this dilution worth the price. Award ceremonies provide an excellent opportunity to recognize publicly an officer's or Sailor's contribution to the command— something that is impossible with the confidential fitness report.

In my experience, selection and screening boards do not pay much attention to awards and decorations unless extraordinary circumstances (usually bravery in action) are involved. A Silver Star, a Navy Cross, and, of course, the Medal of Honor are noted positively. Indeed, Navy Cross and Medal of Honor winners are notable for the rest of their career and admired by their comrades in arms. And sometimes this halo effect carries over to promotion boards. Nonetheless, most senior and retired officers know that many highly decorated naval heroes have not always fared well before such boards. This is not because they did not deserve their decorations but because there is much more to a successful career than serving bravely and well in combat. Some purists may bemoan this fact, arguing that the services are organized and trained for combat and that it is silly to not reward (and promote) those who have been tested in combat and performed well. But they confuse promotions predicated on future service leadership requirements with rewards and awards presented in recognition for past service.

The Navy has attempted, though sometimes unsuccessfully, to separate the award system for bravery and service from the promotion system. I can demonstrate this with a sea story. During the Korean War, I served in a destroyer. My chief gunner's mate had served as a gunner's mate third class before World War II. While in that rate he spent a lot of time in the boxing ring and was once the Pacific Fleet heavyweight boxing champion. We suspected that a proud battleship skipper had given him his crow (petty officer status) for his ring exploits. At any rate, this third-class gunner's mate and boxer was captured by the Japanese early in the war. He was not treated tenderly by his captors. Shortly after the end of the war he was administratively advanced to chief gunner's mate after having worked very little time in his rating. My leadership challenge was to turn this completely unqualified leader—war hero and somewhat punchy former boxer—into a working gunner's mate while my ship was firing more than a thousand rounds a week at North Korean targets. I failed but was spared the consequences because he was medically evacuated with two ruptured eardrums after walking under the gun barrel of a mount engaging the enemy ashore.

In recent years many officers, particularly senior officers with perhaps five or more rows of ribbons, have taken up the practice of wearing only their most senior ribbons—perhaps a single row under their warfare pin. They do this not only for convenience but also to demonstrate that the top decorations say it all without the need for the many campaign and other ribbons that flesh out the decorations resume. Other officers, however, do wear the entire repertoire because they believe that to wear fewer decorations would be to demean any award omitted, an award worn proudly by those who have fewer to wear. In my view, this divide is more a matter of style than substance.

You should not take awards too seriously. If they come your way, accept them graciously and wear them proudly, but understand that most are poor substitutes for an outstanding (e.g., "early promote") fitness report. Awards are the Navy's way of providing visible recognition of superior performance. Your lack of decorations will not be a strike against you because those officers sitting on boards generally recognize that the awards system has had capricious periods and that the awarding authorities are in many cases notoriously fickle and arbitrary. Moreover, awards are often an afterthought, and award citation drafting is frequently left to very junior officers in the command. Some award citations are so carelessly drafted as to be an embarrassment when read at a formal occasion.

For me the most important part of wearing medals and campaign ribbons has nothing to do with performance and promotion. Rather, such awards are a tangible demonstration of the wearer's sea and air service in the conflicts of the cold war and beyond. The World War II and Korean War veterans have retired, and most Vietnam War veterans have joined them. The campaign and battle stars and "Combat Vs" tell the story of active service and identify a band of brothers and sisters with solid bonds to each other, their service, and their country.

15

Pass the (Social) Polish, Please

Manners maketh the man [or woman].
—William of Wykeham

This chapter is about something called social polish—a soft subject to those who might believe that *Animal House* is the standard to be met in public and personal conduct. The topic includes more than "knife-and-fork" etiquette, a jibe from those who see it as a quaint subject far removed from the give-and-take of everyday life. Social polish includes basic courtesy and consideration for others. *You cannot be a gentleman or lady without it.* It is not the sole possession of the well-to-do or the so-called upper social strata. In fact, the affluent are frequently among the most ill mannered of today's Americans, whereas many people from humble backgrounds, the "poor but proud," possess excellent if occasionally old-fashioned manners. And some self-styled aristocrats deliberately and arrogantly comport themselves crudely to demonstrate that the usual rules of polite behavior do not apply to them.

This book is not a volume on etiquette. Many such books exist, and most are good. The point here is that the social graces are among the most valuable tools an officer has—along with professional competence, the art of briefing, the ability to write clear and concise English prose, and so on. The best news is that the social graces comprise an art that can be learned if you were not fortunate enough to get that indoctrination early in your life.

Bad manners are all around us. Simple good table manners seem to be a lost art in some wardrooms and in many restaurants. Although we give our seniors the respect that is their due, though even here some lapses occur, our courtesy to other shipmates regardless of seniority is often deplorable. Today our Navy faces the same challenges in this regard that the Royal Navy faced in the seventeenth century when it was alleged that its officers were not gentlemen and that its gentlemen were not sailors. We run the risk of a descent in our manners to the level of the popular cultural scene. The fact that the Navy is a service of young people, where peer pressure is a critical factor, makes our job to stop the ebb even harder.

To have social graces starts with knowing what the rules are and not ridiculing them as only for the old and out of touch. It means you must not only have an etiquette book in your personal library but also update yourself occasionally on its contents. It is more than a reference book; it is a guide to daily conduct. To have the social graces means to demonstrate by your conduct that you consider others, avoid needless embarrassment, put people at ease, and present an appearance and demeanor that are respectful and attentive to what is going on about you. It means you should avoid the in-your-face confrontations and shouting matches, the put-down styles, and the me-first demeanor so often seen on TV shows and in the movies. Most modern situation comedies present good examples of how *not* to conduct yourself.

Why are these graces important components of a naval officer's seabag? The simple answer is that the more successful you are in your career, the more likely you will be in the public spotlight and the more likely you will represent the United States Navy overseas and before the American public and its representatives. If your behavior is rough, uncouth, and grating and if your manners are deficient, it will reflect adversely on you and the Navy. Consequently, when the Navy picks its future leaders, it pays some attention to the social polish of its candidates. It is not to your advantage to be described as "a bit rough around the edges," "a diamond in the rough," or "not suitable for polite company," or . . . well, you get the idea. Alas, this is not to say that everyone in the Navy's leadership has polished manners. Some manage to climb to the top without them, but their climb was made the more difficult for their rough edges. And when those few get to the top, their lack of polish is a major disadvantage in gaining the respect of others for their office and their service.

How We Arrived Where We Are Today

The Navy of the nineteenth and first half of the twentieth century was an aristocratic service whose officers with few exceptions had meticulous manners. True, officers came from all sorts of social backgrounds, but almost all regular officers graduated from the Naval Academy, and that institution placed great emphasis on social polish. Conforming at the academy was the rule then as it is now, but the standard of social conduct that one was required to conform to was much higher than it has become at the academy, in the naval service, and in society as a whole. In those earlier days you measured up—or else. With the great expansion of the Navy just before and during World War II, the service went through a major transformation, and most peacetime niceties and civilities went by the board. A war was on, and some of its first casualties were the social graces among the officer corps. Not only was the Naval Academy no longer the standard setter in such matters, but many if not most of the new officers brought on for the duration of the war had not finished their college education. Although a college education is not a guarantee of good manners, the experience exposes one to their practice. In the main the wartime officers turned out to be good fighters, and much was forgiven for lapses in the social graces.

When I entered the academy just after World War II, the Navy was still very large, and the push was on to get all officers a college degree. An attempt was also made to resurrect the prewar system of instilling the social graces among midshipmen at the academy. Table manners were emphasized, calls were made and returned, officers were not to be seen pushing baby strollers and using umbrellas, polite social conversation was nurtured, boisterous conduct was frowned on, and junior officers were expected to be attentive to their seniors and not speak up unless called on. But in civil society the postwar assault on good manners overwhelmed even the Naval Academy.

We need to focus on the health of good manners at the Naval Academy because if the academy does not get it right, the chances are that the naval service will not do so either. Setting the tone for the service's officer accession programs is still one of the de facto missions of the academy. The controlled atmosphere at Annapolis provides a major testing ground for making improvements in the officer corps.

This brief look at the historical background is intended to make you more sensitive to where we were and where we are and to provide a personal and institutional incentive to make progress. Social graces are one of the keys to your success in life—in service or in civilian life. You may still engage in the rough-and-tumble and give-and-take of the wardroom, the ready room, the athletic field, and the locker room while paying attention to how ladies and gentlemen behave. We kid a great deal about the point that we are officers and gentlemen (or ladies) by act of Congress. But if you overlook how we conduct ourselves, you will operate your entire career without an important skill.

Ten Simple Rules for Social Acceptability

1. Get an etiquette book and read it. Do it now.
2. Be quiet and listen. Not everyone wants to hear what you have to say. Conversation among ladies and gentlemen is a multisided affair. Listening well is not only an official but also a social necessity.[1]
3. Stand up. This elementary courtesy is the hallmark of a gentleman or lady when addressed by a senior (in rank or age).
4. Defer to others in social matters—in conversation, dining, and precedence. Make the effort to see that others are seated or served first, given the right-of-way, and so on.

5. Pay attention to what is going on around you. You might learn how to conduct yourself and learn what is required. Officers who are unaware are of no use to anyone and a source of embarrassment to their shipmates.

6. Pay attention to your grooming. You should wear a well-turned-out uniform and civilian clothing and maintain hair, nails, and basic body cleanliness.

7. Treat your associates as ladies and gentlemen (even if they are not). Even one or two ladies or gentlemen in a group raise the tone of the gathering.

8. Do not draw attention to yourself—in dress, voice, or actions. Boisterous and exhibitionist behavior does not define the lady or gentleman.

9. Pay attention to your language. You should eliminate not only cursing and profanity but also the crudities in common usage: rough, trendy, "with it" slang. Listen to what you are saying. If you use two to three "you know" expressions a minute in your speech, you have said too much.

10. Do not complain or whine. If you cannot or will not change matters, do not comment on what is wrong with you or the world.

These ten rules, if scrupulously observed, would go a long way to make you a lady or gentleman—whatever the gaps in your upbringing or education or lapses caused by keeping rough company. You will quickly notice that these rules do not apply just to naval officers and might wonder what the connection is to your profession. Part of the answer has been provided earlier: you will be a more respected representative of the Navy at home, abroad, and aboard ship if you are a lady or gentleman and are seen as such by your skippers. The rest of the answer lies in the effect that courteous behavior has on your relationships with your shipmates. You will find that friendship and comradeship come easier even with your enlisted men and women. Some of these individuals may be very crude in manner, but they know a gentleman or lady when they see one, and most instinctively react positively. They quickly perceive that you see beyond yourself and respect them as well. The best of them will want to emulate your behavior, and so an upward spiral in civility, mutual respect, and unit effectiveness occurs.

I once observed a commander (who was soon selected for captain) who was serving as a department head on an aircraft carrier. She was a lady of great charm. She was dignified and treated her Sailors with firmness, respect, and courtesy. She brooked no nonsense but had great warmth of manner based on her being a lady of honor and dignity. Her Sailors would do anything for her, tolerating no disrespect toward her from their shipmates. She was one of the most effective department heads in a ship of outstanding department heads. Her department was consistently the best in the force year after year of her tenure. Social polish and poise are gifts that keep giving and giving. And the best part is that they can be learned, with others helping you in the effort.

16

The Navy Spouse

A naval officer's wife is of great importance to his career, as well as
to the Navy, and indeed in some instances to the United States itself.
—Vice Adm. James Calvert USN (Ret.)

Admiral Calvert wrote the preceding words in the 1960s when the term
"wife" was used to refer to the spouse of a naval officer. In his book *The
Naval Profession,* Calvert reminds us that the role of the wife was so important that space was provided on an officer's fitness report so his senior
could comment on the wife's contribution to the command.[1] Of course,
"spouse" has replaced "wife" in today's usage, and in today's world of husbands and wives in the Navy, working spouses, and increased partition-
ing of social lives from work lives, this now-long-gone practice seems
strange—and objectionable. Moreover, the egalitarian core of our social
fabric resents imposing hierarchical relationships on social interactions.

Junior officer readers may be wondering why this subject is coming
up at all. After all, they will note that so far I have emphasized professional
performance. What does a spouse have to do with such performance? And
why is it that at almost every change of command or retirement ceremony
so much attention is given to spousal and family support? What does such
support have to do with conning a ship, leading a division of enlisted personnel, or flying an airplane? The answers to these and other such questions require stepping back from the specific skills required in the naval
profession and looking at the people serving in ships, in squadrons, and

in the offices of the shore establishment both as human beings and as critical parts of what makes the Navy work. Many of these human beings have spouses and families as well as other outside responsibilities. A naval officer with a chronically unhappy spouse or with family worries is unlikely to be a high-performing officer. And some fit that template and head for the door to civilian life.

Coaches have long known that top performance on the athletic field is keyed to eliminating distractions and fostering a supportive atmosphere in the athlete's family.

Whereas there is game day for athletes, there are overseas deployments for naval officers who leave their families behind. An important part of the readiness equation is to have spouses and families adequately informed and supported—and supportive. Navy spouses themselves play an important role in meeting these requirements.

Although we marry our spouses for other reasons, let me lay out a few of the characteristics of Navy spouses that would be assets to their partner's career.[2]

1. Navy spouses should be blessed with a generally *positive outlook* and a cheerful disposition. They need not be unconditionally optimistic, but they should be willing to give others and circumstances the benefit of the doubt.
2. Navy spouses should be *flexible*. They will encounter many changes in location and circumstances in their spouse's career. They should take pride in their ability to adapt without complaint.
3. Navy spouses should be *problem solvers*. Problems are a fact of life in any marriage. But married life in the Navy involves dealing with surprises (some unpleasant) with the spouse deployed and not available.
4. Navy spouses should be *sociable and caring* and not isolate themselves from others. Empathy is an important characteristic because spouses will often be in a position of providing assistance to or receiving assistance from the families of the command while their spouses are deployed.

5. Navy spouses should *respect* their spouse's career and shipmates. Absence of this respect acts as a corrosive on the unit's cohesiveness and their spouse's effectiveness.

6. Navy spouses should *not be born rebels* or anti-establishment. They need not be conformists, but they must be willing to subordinate their views and conduct in those areas where they interface with their spouse's naval duties and commitments.

7. Navy spouses must be prepared to make *personal sacrifices* to advance their spouse in the profession.

8. Navy spouses should *not wear their spouse's rank*. Although they will enjoy a certain amount of deference and will routinely be treated with great courtesy, they should neither demand nor expect special consideration.

I have observed Navy spouses for more than fifty years, and as a group I admire them immensely. They have been spunky, tough, caring, positive, and loyal to both their spouses and the Navy as an institution. It is no wonder that many if not most Navy personnel who lose their spouse remarry into the service. They understand the pain of loss and the joys of homecomings.

Do some Navy spouses fail to meet these standards? Sure. Some have a great deal of difficulty adjusting to family separations during overseas deployments, to what they see as a hierarchical and inward-looking social life, and to the need to move frequently. Others believe the potential financial advantages of civilian life and the business world outweigh the security that the service provides. Most are decent people whose spouse is in the wrong profession as far as they are concerned. My counsel for those who intend to depart is to go as gracefully as possible with absence of rancor. The Navy families you leave behind have difficult challenges ahead of them, as you well know, and they need your goodwill and best wishes rather than your scorn and elaborate expressions of sympathy.

A question often posed is whether individuals in the Navy get promoted or fail of selection because of their spouse. Some officers who are on the cusp of selection or nonselection may have been pushed over the hump (or down the hill) because of an outstandingly good or problematic spouse. Spouses with a great reputation, that is, spouses who are involved positively, have been a booster and a morale builder in the unit, and have a wide circle of Navy friends, are real pluses, and their virtues are known very widely throughout the service. Yes, spouses have reputations, just as their serving partners do. Spouses who are, for example, troublesome, heavy drinkers, gossips, or militant loners, are a disadvantage to their serving officer. When detailing an officer to an overseas or aide job, the assignment officers will in some cases shade their recommendations for or against the candidate on the basis of their knowledge of a spouse's reputation.

But the principal impact of a spouse's suitability is on the serving officers themselves. A supportive spouse is a priceless asset in boosting an officer's self-confidence, ability to bring focus to the job and the command, and willingness to sign up for the sacrifices that are the hallmark of a successful career. It comes down to the commitment of the spouse to the serving officer and that officer's commitment to a lifetime of service. Just as good husbands and wives anywhere get through the vicissitudes of life as a team, the best Navy spouses serve their partners and their country as teammates.

17

Assignment and Placement Officers

All detailing is local.
—Comdr. Clay Harris, USN

When I was growing up in the Navy, the personnel office was called BuPers or the Bureau of Personnel. Before that it was called the Bureau of Navigation—a not inappropriate name for an organization whose duties included the job of processing officers from assignment to assignment. Today, although there is still a Chief of Naval Personnel, the assignment and placement of officers is done by the Naval Personnel Command in Millington, Tennessee. The assignment and placement (slating) of flag officers, however, is still done in Washington.

The Mechanics

The name, location, and technical support of the business have changed over the years, but the heart of the business has not. Despite gossip to the contrary, the detailers still represent you and with few exceptions try to help you navigate through a succession of assignments that represent a balance between what you want to do, what you should do, and what they (and you) *must* do. Opposite your detailer or assignment officer stands the placement officer. The placement officers represent the commands of the Navy—ships, squadrons, staffs, and shore activities including the various schoolhouses. The business works this way. The placement officers representing the command notices that one of the officers in that command is coming up for rotation. He or she identifies a billet to be filled and a date to fill it. The detailers (assignment officers) pick up on that and go over the list of officers for whom they are responsible to see whether there is a match for a qualified officer (perhaps you) becoming available during that time period.

The match should meet the following criteria: (1) the soon-to-be vacant billet fits with your natural career progression, (2) the timing window works, (3) the proposed assignment is consistent with your preferences (if possible), and (4) your performance record is strong enough to warrant such an assignment. In short, once the detailer is satisfied that you are qualified and available for the billet, that officer markets you to the placement officer.

The placement officer tries to avoid gapping the billet but does want you to have the necessary schooling and training en route to your job. The better your performance record, the easier it is for the assignment officer to market you to the placement officer. Occasionally the receiving command will accept a gap if it means getting a better-suited or quality officer assigned. The tricky part of this process is that no one has a veto—not the assignment officer, not the placement officer, and not you. It is a negotiating process where the leverage of any given player is limited. The placement officer or the receiving command may be given limited choices—perhaps between only two officers—and must consider gapping the billet or accepting a less-qualified officer than they desire. As a junior officer you may not be consulted at all—though in today's Navy a much greater effort is made to satisfy your preferences. If given a choice and you are not willing to accept an assignment that is career enhancing (in the detailer's view), you may have to accept a lesser assignment but one that is more in line with your preferences. At the end of the day, the detailer must fill the soon-to-be vacant billet or persuade the placement officer and the affected command to accept a gap.

One detailer indicates the pitfalls this way:

An officer who fails to screen or promote will often claim after the fact that a low-impact, fur-lined job may have tipped the scales against him at Board

Time. What I have learned is that in most cases, the officer himself went to great lengths to secure that job and took it against his detailer's advice—in some cases with the full blessing and support of his mentor/advisor/sea daddy. What officers may not be aware of is that detailers keep brief electronic records of significant conversations (and e-mail exchanges) with their constituents using screen notes. These notes never go away, unless the detailer erases them. Quite often an assignment officer can look back a few years and find evidence that LCDR Smith knew he was taking an assignment against the advice of his then-detailer, that the job would likely be perceived as detrimental to his upward mobility.[1]

Officers are expected to keep a current Duty Preference Card on file with their detailer. Woe unto officers with weak or mediocre records who do not have their cards on file and who fail to engage their detailer when coming into the assignment window. More than one such "disengaged" officer has been surprised by a set of orders to a distant, exotic, or peculiar duty station. If you do not have a current Duty Preference Card, you are telling the detailer that you do not care where you go.

The arithmetic of the detailing process is such that there are always more billets than officers to fill them. The reasons for this are complex but are rooted in fact that pipelines are always longer than the budgeted number of bodies to fill them. People represent money, and Congress grants money on the basis of its perception of what the officer strength of the Navy and the efficiency of its assignment process should be. But as I have indicated throughout this book, some billets are less desirable than others but are still important enough for some officers to be ordered to fill them. A numbers game soon transforms into a quality (of performance) game, a clout game (some commanders bring more leverage to the assignment process), and a game involving your willingness to trade off one preference (e.g., a step up the command preparation pyramid) for another (e.g., your desire for a particular locality). Throughout this process an emphasis is placed on filling sea billets at the expense of shore billets.

All this is a brokering process whose object is to fill as many billets with as many qualified officers who are satisfied with their assignments as possible. It is not an easy business, and the detailers are at the pointed end of a difficult process. Some call them "flesh peddlers" because they are indeed marketers—selling the placement officers on your fitness for the jobs on offer and selling you on the benefits of the job for your career or in meeting your other preferences. And they have a full set of sales pitches to smooth the process. Let us discuss a few of them.

"We need your expertise in the job."
In this pitch the detailer emphasizes your experience in a similar job and the need for it in a follow-on job. In this formulation you are a pro whose abilities are badly needed in the open billet. On the other hand, if you have never been in a similar assignment before, the detailer may pitch it by saying, "You need to broaden your area of expertise to become promotable or more assignable downstream." The second pitch was used to get an officer into the personnel business on her second shore tour, and the first pitch was used to get her into two follow-on tours in the personnel business—even though her subspecialty and postgraduate education were in politico-military affairs. Both pitches are legitimate and even honest, but you have to decide whether you want to buy the argument and what you can do about it if it is not what you want.

"This job requires a high-performing officer."
This pitch is not only to your ego but also to get you into a billet that demands a high performer. The detailer is telling you that the placement officer will not accept just anybody to fill the open billet. The implication is that the billet is a plus in your career planning. But the detailer may also be telling you that you may be put in with a group of highly motivated individuals where the competition will be fierce (which is not all bad).

"This job calls for an officer in the grade of [the next highest rank]."
This pitch means that no qualified officer was available at the higher grade to fill the billet. You should ask why. Chances are that it is a less-desirable billet at that grade and that they had a hard time finding an officer to fill it. Therefore, the system has downshifted to fill it. This can be an opportunity, but it is just as likely that the billet has been misgraded.

Another possibility is that the receiving command would rather have a more junior but higher quality officer (you) than another more senior but less competitive officer offered by the detailers. You have to ask yourself whether serving in the billet on offer would be career enhancing. Remember, too, that billets can be downgraded to the next lower rank while you are serving in it.

"You were recommended (or asked for) to fill this billet."
This sales pitch is another appeal to your ego. Being asked for is nice, but is this a job that fits in with your progression to screening for command? How will it look to a promotion board? The people who asked for you or recommended you will not be identifiable to or known by the boards—unless the billet is a high-visibility one (in which case there is no problem). A variant of this pitch is that you are among two or three nominees for the job—and the nominees are well known to you to be high performers.

"Your timing is great."
In this pitch the detailer knows you are coming up before a screening or promotion board (say in the next year) and that the job on offer will enhance your resume. In a variation of this pitch, the detailer will say that the boss is well known and that it would be in your interest to have a fitness report signed by that individual before the board meets. Another variation is that you will get to the command just before it deploys and hence will get valuable experience and a chance for a more impressive fitness report. There are many other variations of this game. It is like timing the stock market to

buy or sell. You can get stung badly if you are wrong in the face of a fickle future. Remember: job first, timing second.

"You need more operational experience."
This statement may be true, but some operational experiences are better than others. To go to sea and be put on a deployable staff is helpful in one way, but if it delays assignment to a department head or command track billet, it is not as good as a ship or squadron billet.

"You have been selected for postgraduate instruction."
This may be just what you want. To be selected (meaning you made the cut) and to have an opportunity to earn a degree and to have some shore duty after an arduous sea tour can sound great. But be careful. Is that what you really want to do? Getting an advanced degree indicates one or two payback assignments are in your future. Are those payback tours likely to be in career-enhancing jobs? The Navy needs postgraduate-educated officers, but is that the turn you want to take? This topic was discussed earlier when we examined the place of the schoolhouse in your career progression. Your decision needs some hard thinking.

"We need you back ashore."
The implication is that you have been at sea or in command long enough and that it is time to give others a chance. Never be talked into leaving a sea command early, no matter who wants you. You should leave command kicking and screaming. A year in command simply is not long enough to learn the business. Two years is both better and a minimum, in my view. If your shortened tour contained an overseas deployment, you can rest somewhat easier. But the threat of being ripped out just before a deployment should send you to battle stations. Rip outs are normally the result of high-level attention in the Naval Personnel Command or in the office of the Chief of Naval Operations. Your presence is demanded now, and there may be little that you can do about it. The detailer may head you off by telling you, "Do

not fight these orders because the guys who decide these matters have already decided." But before rolling over, check with the officer who is demanding you to see whether that was the intention—or that you are being rolled. Sometimes you will be ripped out to relieve an officer who has received a high-priority assignment. You are at the end of a daisy chain.

"This is a joint [or combined] billet."[2]

Here the detailer will point out, if you do not already know it, that joint or combined duty is a prerequisite for selection to flag rank.[3] But the type of billet (is it with the J-3 in the Joint Staff of the Joint Chiefs of Staff or in a small joint technical field activity?) and the timing (should you be at sea at this point?) are important factors. Keep your eye on your objective: qualifying for command at sea. Your flag hurdles should take second in priority behind getting ready for command. That said, you would have a leg up in flag selection if you have already had your joint tour.

"You need the flight hours."

This ploy is normally used with aviators who are to be ordered to flying billets ashore. You may need the flight hours—or at least they would help you as you go up the ladder and strive to screen for squadron command. But a prior question is, why did you not get the needed hours in an earlier tour? I know of very few officers whose career was salvaged by going to instructor duty to pile up flight hours. Another prior question should be, why are they not sending you as a replacement air group instructor instead? It may be that your performance record is not good enough to qualify for assignment to the RAG as an instructor. This is how less than great performance can hurt you in the assignment process. It is not enough to get to good billets; you must perform well while there.

"You are going as an aide to the admiral."

Many years ago flag lieutenants were designated as staff communicators. These days flag lieutenants (at sea) and aides (ashore) are more the personal assistants than key members of the staff. They are seldom involved with the substance of the staff's business. Rarely would an admiral ask an aide's opinion on a major matter of substance in making a decision. Aide jobs can be good jobs, but not for the reasons you may think. You may think that you can do no wrong to be working directly for an admiral. You may think that the admiral may be able to help you with getting a plum follow-on assignment. This is wrong thinking, however. An aide's job is good to the degree that you get a broader appreciation of what the Navy is about. You see the decisions your admiral is called on to make. You begin to realize that the Navy is more than a chain of command. You probably will gain some social polish. But the content of most aide jobs is more menial than that. These jobs involve scheduling, travel arrangements, honors, office management, and so on. You will find yourself a mess caterer, a valet, and a fixer, not a key adviser at the right hand of someone at the top.

Moreover, your admiral almost surely will be long retired before that individual would have influence (if any) for the critical milestones for your career. I had one aide tour and one executive assistant (senior aide) tour in my career, and although I learned much in those tours, they did not smooth my path to command. They did, I believe, make me a better skipper once I got there. My advice is to go into an aide tour with your eyes wide open. Filling the job does not mean you are one of the anointed; it is an interesting detour as you prepare yourself for command. If you have any control in the matter, do not stay in the job long. In a year you can learn most of what there is to learn.

"There are a lot of perks with the job."
You do not hear this as much today. In days past, a captain stationed in command overseas might have a number of perks: a personal auto and driver, special allowances, government quarters, household help—and even a personal aircraft and crew in some overseas assignments. At one time there was a billet at a South American war college where the incum-

bent was paid not only his U.S. service pay but also (and legally) the pay of an equivalent officer in the host navy.

Today the perks are more modest and in most cases limited to a few overseas jobs. In my experience an officer who took a job for the perks was not a front-runner. That officer was simply making the best of a career that was already terminal. It is axiomatic today that a good career job has terrible hours, family separation, no government quarters, some personal danger, a great deal of workplace pressure to produce, and often is located in a threatening neighborhood—or all of the above.

"This is a new (and important?) billet."
Billets are being established and disestablished daily. Just because the billet is new does not mean it is on the career main line. Many such billets are highly specialized, and their importance may be fad related. The Navy has fads as does any large organization. Special program billets can be very trendy and tricky, so buyer beware.

The Placement Officer

We now turn to the other half of the assignment equation, the placement officer. You will not have much to do with placement officers until you become an XO or a staff personnel officer. As indicated earlier, placement officers are the command's window into the personnel assignment world. The placement officer's job is to fill the client command's billets with qualified relief and no gaps. If time permits, the placement officer will confer with the command before accepting candidates for their billets. Because some officer types are in short supply (e.g., post command commanders), some billets will be gapped, filled with more junior (or in some cases more senior) officers or with officers without the necessary credentials of education, warfare qualifications, and so on.

Before one places too many demands on placement officers, remember that by definition almost half the Navy's officers are below the servicewide performance average. This does not mean that such officers cannot do the job—just that they are not the hottest runners and in most cases need not be to do a good job. It is natural to want the best, but wisdom may lie in the recognition that the best are not always necessary. Indeed, they may cause the command a problem both at fitness report time and in keeping the peace in the wardroom, ready room, or flag mess. You want the best officers for only the very best jobs.

Misconceptions about the Officer Personnel System

There is a widespread perception that favoritism pervades the Navy's personnel assignment and placement systems.[4] This perception is fostered by the fact that some officers do not get the assignments they want and believe they deserve and that somebody else got the desired job. The systems are run by human beings, and they deal in a human product. It is not surprising that misperceptions and disappointments occur. Some very senior officers do attempt to manipulate the system, for example, a call to the detailer or placement officer's boss or his boss. Some senior officers get their way. And this is not always bad. Any personnel system should strive to be fair, but it should also be responsive to the needs of top management.

What keeps the system fair? First, the detailers have available to them a numerical readout on how you stack up with your contemporaries. Although the gradations may be fine and arguable at the margin, detailers will have a good idea as to how competitive you are and whether you are in the hunt for command screening and promotion. If you have screened they will know your ranking in the screening. They also have your preference card at hand. But more important than that is the fact that the receiving commands want the best, and it is not to their advantage to accept less than the best when the best are available. *If you have an excellent record, you will get a good job because it is in the self-interest of the system and its players to get you into one.*

Does it happen that sometimes a less-than-the-best officer gets the best job? It does occur, but not very often. Senior officers, in picking an executive assistant, are sometimes willing to accept less than the best (though few will admit it) in order to get someone they know in the billet that involves daily personal contact. Four-star officers, as senior members of the Navy's board of directors, get considerable latitude in picking their key staff members. But in observing the system at work for many years and seeing first-hand what goes on, I believe the system is as fair as human ingenuity can make it. This explanation will not satisfy the disappointed candidates who were not selected. But they and their supporters err in my view when they transform personal disappointments into a judgment of systemic weakness.

Dealing with Your Detailer

Keep the relationship between you and the detailer professional. Detailers have a job to do, and you do, too. Do not be afraid to ask them how you stack up, whether the prospective assignment fills your career needs, what the alternatives are, what negotiating room there is on timing, what schools can be attended en route, and under ideal circumstances what your follow-on assignment should be. They should also be apprised of any special circumstances in your assignment (e.g., a special-education child, a working spouse, an impending divorce, or major illness). In my experience too many officers take on an adversarial relationship with their detailers. A detailer may never be your friend but can and should be your professional adviser. You may respond that it is not your job to solve their problems, particularly if solving them is at your professional expense. This is true, but there is room for courtesy and negotiation, gently pressing the envelope, understanding the give-and-take of the process, and working toward an acceptable if not optimal solution.

Some very senior officers I know are proud of the fact that they never challenged a proposed assignment. The assignment ended up challenging them. Because they were very successful, they tended to go to the top jobs anyway. But if you are frequently in the position of having to challenge the detailer's judgment or candor, you should start to ask yourself whether you stack up in professional performance. The best officers do not have to argue for the top assignments. Those who are a step below them and are striving for the top rung are the ones who have the most difficult road. It all goes back to your performance—which is where this book started. This is not to say that a healthy skepticism is not warranted, only to say that the system does pretty well without a lot of self-interested tinkering.

Your assignment dilemmas will include the following:

1. Whether or when to attend a war college or a postgraduate course of instruction. The latter in particular can have a profound effect on your career.
2. Whether to take a somewhat cushy billet that fits in with your family and life objectives or elect to follow the path through the school of hard knocks (deployments, family separation, and perhaps homeports with substandard public schools).
3. Whether to jump from one warfare or subspecialty track to another.
4. Where and what billet to go to on shore duty.
5. Determining when a projected assignment or your failure to screen is so unacceptable (in your eyes) that you consider resignation or retirement.
6. Whether to extend your tour in any given billet (you may have no choice).
7. Whether to feather your nest for a future retirement (billets or education that enhance your resume) or stay in the screening and promotion races.

One of the principal purposes of the book before you is to give you the necessary background to answer these questions. But such information and advice are useless unless you deal honestly with yourself in appraising your capabilities and shortcomings. We will return to this subject in the last chapter. Now it is time to look at the fitness report system.

18

The Fitness Report System

Carry out every assignment to the best of your ability. There is no
better or faster way to "break out of the pack" than to establish a
reputation for reliable and timely performance.

—Rafael C. Benitez, *Anchors: Ethical and Practical Maxims*

This chapter kicks off our discussion of the mechanics of promotion. But
do not look here for details contained in the most recent instructions
from the Department of the Navy. Those you can check for yourself. What
you should look for in the discussion that follows are enduring principles, not how you would like to have your boss fill in the boxes on the current fitness report form. That said, we will use current fitness report directives as a backdrop for our narrative.[1]

In its fundamentals, a fitness report is in five parts:

1. Duties Assigned
2. Command Employment and Command Achievements
3. Performance Traits (e.g., Leadership and Tactical Performance)
4. Comments on Performance (a narrative).
5. Promotion Recommendations

The last three parts are most important because those are the areas where
the seniors do their heavy lifting. Under recent changes to fitness report
directives, explicit comparisons and breakouts ("number one of five

department heads," for example) are permitted and expected. Reporting seniors who do not break out their players on the back of the report place them at risk. This "Promotion Recommendations" part of the fitness report format and associated instructions have been the object of a great deal of tinkering over the years. I will address this subject in more detail later in the chapter. For now, there are three things you can be certain of as your career progresses: (1) the format of the fitness report will change, (2) some form of comparison or distribution of officers of similar rank and career path will be required, and (3) skippers will hate to be forced to choose between two or more good officers at fitness report time. For you junior readers, welcome to an organization that, regardless of tales and jibes to the contrary, does change and sponsors and benefits from a career horse race among its cohorts of officers of different ranks and career paths.

Timing of Fitness Reports

In its essentials, there are four types of regular fitness reports:[2]

1. Periodic reports once a year
2. Detachment of your reporting senior
3. Your detachment from the command
4. Special reports intended to cover a variety of narrowly defined unusual circumstances (see BUPERS Instruction 1610.10, p. D-3)

On reports submitted prior to January 1, 1996, there were opportunities for tinkering with the timing, most of it oriented to attempting to "game" the comparative ranking system then in use. Commanding officers had considerable latitude (up to three months) in combining regular and detachment reports. Use of that prerogative permitted a "reluctant to choose" skipper to remove the officer reported on from the comparative ranking system on the officer's detachment. Thus, an officer who might otherwise have been ranked 3 of 7 could be ranked 1 of 1 on his or her detachment date. There were other subterfuges to avoid difficult choices and to reward good performing officers who were not getting a top comparative ranking.

For reports submitted after January 1, 1996, officers are to be counseled on their performance midway through the regular report interval so that they have time to remedy any defects in performance before the actual report is prepared. They are again counseled just before the report is sent to the Naval Personnel Command for recording. The officer reported on is required to sign the report. Most seniors do not write up shortcomings unless they are gross. Less-than-gross shortcomings are reserved for the oral counseling. One skipper tells his officers that those individuals reported on are little more than an "info addressee" on a fitness report. Nothing in a report should be a surprise if the reporting senior has exercised the degree of leadership the Navy expects of that individual. The same skipper goes on to say, "A fitness report is neither a reward nor a form of punishment; it is a tool designed to capture as succinctly as possible that officer's potential for further service and to convey to an anonymous selection board what that officer is capable of doing for the Navy."

Narrative Comments on Performance

Long fitness report narratives are not desired. The narrative is intended to back up with concrete facts and examples the grading contained elsewhere in the report. This section gives the specifics that cannot be described by checking the boxes in the report. Many skippers use the narrative as an opportunity to converse with future screening and selection boards. But that conversation is terse and to the point. Some skippers use the narrative to reduce the sting administered elsewhere in the report where tough choices have to be made. Most skippers make the narrative a combination art form and sales pitch. They are very sensitive to the fact that they are talking to three audiences simultaneously: the Naval Personnel Command that is in charge of quality control for the fitness report system, future selection and screening boards, and the officer being reported on. Each audience is looking for something different: that the reporting rules are being observed, that the skipper is being candid and forthcoming with future board members, and that you (the officer being reported on) are being treated fairly with a proper balance between your strengths and shortcomings, if any.

The quality-control authorities have a number of prohibitions to rein in the too-enthusiastic commanding officer. But the most important weapons in the quality-control locker are (1) the quota controls on the award of "early promote" and "must promote" recommendations in each group of reports on officers in specific "officer competitive categories," and (2) the comparison of the trait mark average on your report with the summary group average (your competition in the command) now required by the fitness report form.

The current system is based on four pillars:

1. Ranking of an officer is compared across promotion recommendation categories (i.e., early promote, must promote, promotable, progressing, and significant problems).
2. A system of constraints and incentives for reporting officers wherein grade inflation is kept under some control (e.g., numerical limits on top promotion recommendation numbers, assigning a grade to raters based on the aggregate of their rating distributions).
3. A concerted effort to make performance reporting an integrated and consistent system (e.g., greater precision in report formats, more specific instructions for compliance, quality-control mechanisms).
4. Counseling is built into the system from the outset. The system is more than a performance recording system; it has mechanisms to encourage awareness of shortcomings and to provide incentives for improvement.

You may ask what all this means for you. It means that you have a better chance than formerly of being treated fairly, knowing where you must improve, gauging your "promotability," removing some of the previous mystery associated with the process, and having the certainty of face-to-face counseling with your supervisors. Commanding officers must make difficult choices openly and are denied the opportunity of gaming the system (or seeing it gamed by other commanding officers). Moreover, grading by commanding officers is the subject of greater institutional scrutiny because the raters' grading tendencies are made more visible. Board members have to work harder than in the old days. The narratives must be read more closely to assess performance differences among officers in the same promotion category. On the other hand, board members have more tools available with a more-precise fitness report format and the means to understand better how given commanding officers are rating their officers (by comparing individual and commandwide trait averages). Now let us turn to how the fitness reports and the various reports that summarize them are used by the boards and assignment officers.

Boards Read the Tea Leaves

As I have observed, periodic efforts are made to "reform" the system. In part these efforts are the result of frustration by screening and selection boards as they attempt to filter out the extraneous, the trivial, the routine, and the puffery put in the reports by some commanding officers. In too many cases, board members must take on the role of detectives, trying to ascertain what your reporting senior *really* meant. A tension exists between the roles of reporting seniors and board members. Commanding officers want to keep their wardroom morale high by giving good (or better) fitness reports as they urge officers on to top performance. Because they counsel their officers and because these officers see their fitness reports, seniors feel an obligation to be both candid and laudatory. In my experience of reading countless fitness reports (and writing a good many), the natural tendency is to overdo praise and soften criticism. Unfortunately, this tendency tends to lull some average or below-average officers into an unwarranted sense of security. I will have more to say on this point at the end of the chapter.

The screening and promotion boards have to sift through all the words, markings, and rankings and pick the very best. Typical commanding officers and their fitness reports make the boards' job very difficult, and, unfortunately, some boards do not always get it right. Some commanding officers believe more is better than less when it comes to writing a fitness report, a practice that puts additional obstacles in the way of understanding. These facts of life have forced boards to rely heavily on comparative rankings—where the writer-skipper must finally declare who is the best or among the best, next best, and so on. But skippers do not give up easily and do their best to avoid being put in a corner.

What You Want the Fitness Report to Say

You want your fitness report to say the following:

1. *You held a demanding job and did so for a protracted period.* Many commanding officers realize that in writing up their department heads they must get every eligible officer into a department head job—even if only briefly—so that every qualified officer has a chance when that individual's record appears before the XO and CO screening boards. Others cut right to the heart of the challenge and put the best officers in the best jobs—and keep them there.
2. *You did so while deployed.* You were tested in a demanding environment, and the fitness report narrative states the salient details of the deployment and your role in it.
3. *You performed well compared to your contemporaries* in similarly demanding jobs. A mark in the "must promote" box is acceptable until you can further prove you have the right stuff to make the "early promote" box.
4. *The narrative supports with facts the quality of your accomplishments.*[3]

5. *You are qualified for the next step in your career progression,* such as department head, executive officer, commanding officer, or major command.

Although your fitness report principally documents your *past performance,* it should also forecast your *future promise.* You perform well not only for the satisfaction of doing a good job but also because that performance is a partial predictor of your future performance in positions of higher responsibility. Your fitness report is intended to speak to future screening and promotion boards, not the historical researcher or the record keeper. The whole report must be forward looking, using past performance as one indicator. The other indicators are your intellectual capacity, your suppleness of mind, your ability to learn from experience and observation, and your suitability for professional growth. As important as these other indicators are, they are crucially affected by proven performance.

Fashioning this linkage between the past and the future is the job of the screening and promotion boards. They can do no better than the raw materials they must work with, meaning principally your reports of fitness. Remember that the members of the boards who judge your suitability have been where you want to go. They know what it takes, and they are looking for what you have to offer that fits the requirement template. But their perspective must look through your promotion jacket and its fitness reports. In a sense your former skippers are their guides in making this assessment.

Danger Signals in Your Fitness Report

You will have an opportunity to read your fitness report and ask your skipper questions about it. Look especially for qualifiers that sound good but on closer examination pull the punch on an evaluation. Such qualifiers include: "One of the best officers in this command," "Usually performs well," "Can be depended on," and "Does assigned tasks well."

Another danger signal is a lack of specificity in the report. The use of general descriptors suggests that your skipper either does not know you (and consequently your performance) very well and is padding the report or is feeding the board (and you) pablum that says pass on a pass/fail test but does not tell you why (or whether) you are better than your running mates. Some commanding officers use general descriptors of praise as a substitute for criticism. A variant of the general (and not very useful) descriptor is the presentation of irrelevant material: "He likes his job" (so what?). "She works hard" (with little effect?). "He boosts ward-room morale" (life of the party?—see chapter 6). "She has a sense of humor" (how does that help the command and her performance?). "He is a good administrator" (also a good operator and maintainer?).

Sometimes there will be veiled criticism in the fitness report. "He reacts positively to suggestions." "He learns quickly with experience." "He has lost weight and is now in good physical condition." "With his current upward trend in performance I believe he will soon be a superb performer." Comments of this type should prompt a discussion with your executive officer or commanding officer to get specifics and to find out in concrete terms what more they expect of you or where you have not met their standards.

What Boards Are Looking for in the Fitness Report Narrative

Boards are looking for concrete evidence of achievement, examples that make a point in your favor (or against), and tangible evidence that your performance is superior to your peers. Notice the specifics in the exemplar comments that follow.

"Performed both regular duties and those as acting XO for two months while regular XO hospitalized; maintained effectiveness and morale in the command and in her department."

"Was first first-tour aviator arriving on this turn-around cycle to become fully weapons qualified. His landing grades were the best for his rank in the squadron."

"Was most junior officer to become fully qualified officer of the deck (OOD) underway (formation) in command during this reporting cycle. Executed an effective and safe emergency breakaway from oiler during an actual steering casualty."

"Although her squadron is not yet best in the air wing, it is the most improved, and she would be my first choice to relieve my deputy CAG if the need arose."

"Have deliberately loaded him up with a myriad of extra duties beyond his billet and pay grade for the simple reason that under pressure he is the most effective officer in the command and is absolutely dependable. Is the 'go to guy' in the command."

"Knows more about the installed weapons system than anyone in the command, including her chief petty officers and me. Reduced CASREP rate for systems in her department by half with no change in supply priorities. The one indispensable person serving in this ship."

Your Input to Your Fitness Report

Your commanding officer is required under current directives to obtain your input to your upcoming fitness report. Your input will be in the form of an information sheet that can be used as a basis for documenting your performance. Sometimes this is a simple listing of duties performed, qualifications gained, off-duty education completed, next duty preferences, and so on. But with care you can go beyond that and provide some detail that may at first glance seem trivial to you but will catch your skipper's eye.

Ask yourself what changes you have made in your division or area of responsibility since you took over. If there are tangible and beneficial results to those changes, tell your bosses what they are. Ask yourself what steps you have taken to qualify yourself for your boss's job. This may be as simple as standing in for that officer when absent or taking on a special project for the person, a project that might get lost in the larger overview your bosses have. Have you kept an "attaboy" file or a file that contains all the "Bravo Zulus" (Well done!) your shop has received? Fitness report time is the time to trot them out and append them to your data sheet—even if your skipper or XO has already seen them. Look over the records kept by your division/shop to see if any data there support uptrends in performance for which you have some responsibility.

You should also be aware that you can do even more to document your performance beyond lists and facts. Append a narrative summary to your fitness report input that weaves the facts together and is crafted in such a way that your senior could, if so inclined, lift sentences and paragraphs out of it for placement in the finished report. You may be doing your senior and yourself a favor—and polishing your writing skills along the way. This is not self-promotion; it is completed staff work.

Trends

Some of you will become discouraged because you seem to be in "the pack." That is, your performance as documented in your fitness reports does not show you breaking out to the "must promote" or "early promote" categories. Note, however, that selection and screening boards are intensely interested in trends. For example, if in a two-year tour under two skippers you get two "promotable" ratings, followed by a "must promote" rating, followed in turn by an "early promote" rating, I guarantee you will have the full attention of board members. You are by definition a late bloomer, and in my experience, boards love late bloomers. Trends (up or down) are very important. Changes in your promotion recommendation across skippers are also important. These changes are even more important when your new and old skippers have a significant variance in their commandwide grade average. The point is that if you are lower than you want to be or think you should be, that should be your first topic in your counseling session with the boss. Catch that updraft! Better yet, make it yourself.

There is a good chance you will get a "farewell bouquet" from your skipper when you are detached. It is that person's chance to put you 1 of 1 in the "early promote" category of your detachment report. But if your earlier reports have placed you in the pack, this farewell kudo loses its punch. And anything less than the best marks in your detachment report could send a negative signal to your next selection or screening board. Do not be lulled into a sense of complacency by the glow of a hand-tooled report that is looking only at you and not at the competition.

The Lure of Self-Delusion

In conjunction with the thought just expressed above, never forget that life is a competitive business, whether in civilian life or in the service. To be "the best" by definition implies ranking and competition. If you selectively listen to and read words of praise but tune out the background, you are setting yourself up for future disappointment. As I have said before in this book and will say again, situational awareness is a prime attribute of successful naval officers. If you are in the pack (as defined by the relevant fitness reports) and stay in the pack over time, at some point you are going to fail to screen or be selected for promotion. All the nice words and reassurances of friends, mentors, and your COs are not going to save you from that disappointment if your fitness reports do not show you breaking out. It is not enough to think, "I have done all they have asked of me." You must do better than that and demonstrate that you are in the front rank of those being screened for command or selected for promotion.

Most failures to screen or be promoted can be traced back to less-than-above-average performance. The complaints and excuses that define the aftermath of that disappointment can in turn be laid at the doorstep of self-delusion. It is rarely "the system's" fault if you miss the hurdle, though it is a convenient scapegoat. If you pay attention to the emerging pattern in your fitness reports over time, you will see the first signs of success or disappointment. Your job is to influence the trend if you wish to progress in your naval career. I have more to say on this subject in appendix A. Competing ably and fairly is the definition of success in the Navy.

Some Administrative Remarks

You do not have to go to the Naval Personnel Command in Millington, Tennessee, to view the most important parts of your promotion jacket or your performance summary report (PSR). You can do most of it at your own personal computer. Just ask Naval Personnel Command to send you a CD with the necessary information tailored to your record. Ask your detailer if you do not know where to start.

Your responsibility goes beyond reviewing the material received, however. Conceivably there are gaps in continuity in your fitness report stream. Perhaps a report from your command (old or current) did not find its way to the Naval Personnel Command. Perhaps there is an unintended gap in the continuity of reports. Every day in your career must be accounted for. It is up to you to bring the errors or omissions to the attention of your command, the Naval Personnel Command, or both. You are both the first and final quality-control officer for your promotion jacket—both as to content and compliance.

19

Screening and Promotion Boards
And the Verdict Is . . .

The best news that you will ever receive is that you screened for
command.
—Anonymous naval aviator

The mechanics of promotion boards are fairly straightforward. The records
of all eligible officers are assembled and reviewed by the boards. One or
two members of the board will be assigned to summarize and brief each
record to the entire board.[1] Then, in secret, members will vote electron-
ically by pushing a button. Often a large number of votes are taken until
the field is winnowed down to the finalists. Then the remaining records
are again briefed to the board (by different briefers), and votes are again
taken until the final and authorized number is selected.

Promotion boards are statutory boards whose status and authority
are determined by law. They are established and provided guidance
under the direction of the Secretary of the Navy, and the boards answer
to that individual, not anyone else in the department. The Secretary provides guidance letters ("precepts") to the boards that state inter alia how
many officers to select and the skills and characteristics wanted in the
selectees. The Secretary does not have the authority to tell the board
members who to select. The Secretary's authority is to approve or dis-
approve the boards' results or, in rare cases, to strike selectees off the list
for a specific reason.

Screening boards are administrative boards in that they are ordered by the commander of the Naval Personnel Command. Practices vary, but screening boards are used primarily to select candidates for executive officer and commanding officer. In some cases even department heads are so selected. Screening boards follow most of the same procedures as promotion boards. They have numbers of selectees specified in the convening letter, but they also may have included numbers for specified subcommunities within a warfare community. The screening boards serve as a critical way station on the career track. In my experience, faring well before screening boards is just as important as promotion boards in your career progress. Screening boards provide you with a ticket to the game. Promotion boards ratify whether you have done a good job in using that ticket.

Members of promotion boards will be drawn from across warfare communities in proportionate numbers to the entire population.[2] Screening board composition, however, is entirely from your warfare community (e.g., aviation, surface warfare, submarine, special warfare). Members of the board will be at least one rank senior to the candidates before the board. The president of the flag promotion board is a four-star officer and is assisted by two or more three-star officers and several two-star officers.

Between summarizing and briefing activities that culminate in the board's voting, there is much discussion among members of the board concerning qualifications of the officers being considered. Some records are so outstanding and the officers' professional reputation so striking that they are selected early in the process. Another group is comprised of officers who have experienced chronic career difficulties and are poor prospects for promotion. In the middle—typically 50 percent or more of the officers examined—the judgments are harder, and the pool receives much closer scrutiny. The "finals" in the deliberative process are a soul-searching exercise for board members. Would I want to have this officer serve under me? What is that officer's skipper really saying? What is left unsaid? What was the competition in that command (sometimes the board finds the answer to that question because the candidate's competitors are often before the same board)? Does this officer show future promise beyond a good record of past performance? Is the officer a candidate to enter the pool of future candidates for flag (in the case of the captain promotion board and major command screening board)? Has this officer taken the easy path, or has the individual been severely tested in areas of high professional risk?

In one key way promotion boards are different from screening boards. Promotion boards consider not only those officers in the promotion zone but also those in the eligibility zone. An officer in the promotion zone who is not selected is considered to have failed of selection ("passed over"), whereas an officer who is merely eligible from below the zone has one or more additional chances before being considered passed over. An officer who is passed over enters special career status. A second pass over is usually the person's ticket to civilian life—either retirement or release from active duty.[3]

The Navy's practice on early promotions (selection from below, junior to, the promotion zone) varies from time to time. Under some Navy Secretaries and circumstances an emphasis is made on getting new blood by promoting more officers earlier. At other times, the question of seasoning and fairness to those in the zone takes precedence. At any rate, the numbers of officers selected early are small—and the accolade great for those who achieve it. To be selected early marks you as a standout in your profession and destined for good jobs and high rank if you keep up the level of your performance. Yet it is also a fact of life that many officers who reach flag rank were never selected early for anything. If you are not selected early, you are still very much in the race. If you are selected early, you have been given a major compliment, and much is expected of you. But humility is also called for because you know the race does not always go to the swift. The line between show horses and workhorses can be exceedingly narrow.

Boards are directed to select on the basis of the record (not service reputation). Yet it is impossible not to be influenced by the service reputation of a candidate before the board and of the senior who signed the reports of fitness. Board members are careful not to influence deliberations by personal biases or preferences. But when a board is groping for fuller knowledge about a candidate, a member who can clarify the point will step up and try to clear the air based on personal knowledge. When this is done, caveats and qualified statements are usually used. In my experience and in almost all cases, at least one member of the board knows either the candidate or the senior who signed important reports of fitness. There are few mystery candidates or reporting seniors.

Personal knowledge of a candidate, knowledge that could be considered adverse, cannot be discussed unless the information appears in the eligible member's official record. This guidance is strictly enforced during board proceedings.

The boards meet in private, and the results of the boards are not to be announced before the secretary or other convening authority acts on the recommendations. No contact is allowed between board members or recorders and persons whose jackets are before the board. Some board members, however, have made a discrete phone call to others during recesses to clear up some uncertainty that if left unresolved could do the Navy or the individual great harm.

Even though the deliberations of the boards are strictly private and leaks are expressly prohibited, some information occasionally gets out: "You were in the finals." "One fitness report really hurt." "You need another deployed fitness report." "You are in a good position for the next board." "A couple of board members were not convinced; they wanted to see more sea experience." "I pushed for you as hard as I could, but the field was exceptionally strong. You were competitive but needed something more to push you over the top."[4] Unfortunately, the current long delay between the time the board reports out and the results are published (often three to five months for flag boards) results in more leaks than previously.[5]

Most screening boards rank their selectees to help the detail and placement officers in filling the various slates. Occasionally, officers at the bottom of the list will be "descreened" in a subsequent screening because changed circumstances have made the targeted billets unavailable (e.g., unplanned ship retirements). Just because you have screened does not mean you stay screened. You will be reviewed again the following year if you are not in a billet for which you screened. Some of the most rancorous discussions between senior detailers and screened officers occur when an officer for some reason has experienced descreening. There is the perception of favoritism in spite of the fact that screeners are ranked and that the bottom screeners are the first bumped and get the less-than-most-desirable slots.

Another source of rancor in major command screening is the split between the shore and sea command lists, with the latter being the most desirable. The screening board makes a major effort to ensure balance in quality between the two lists. All the candidates are strong, but some have better seagoing credentials than others do, and the split is up to each board. I know of no way to get changed from one list to another unless the number of respective billets has changed between successive boards.

Because of the decline in ship and squadron numbers that has occurred in the past two decades, more command screened officers are being ordered to shore commands and to commands not always considered at the top rung (e.g., recruiting command slots, fleet shore activities). Still another source of problems is the apportionment of desirable command billets across warfare communities. Boards do not do this, but the split affects the boards. Apportionment has in recent years particularly affected assignment of command of large amphibious ships (LHA and LHD) and logistic support ships.

I will offer a piece of advice here. As you go up the promotion ladder, keep a sharper eye on command screening than on promotion boards. Screening boards are made up of officers from your warfare community, and they know not only the community but also the people (including your skipper) who serve in it. Both a good fitness report jacket and a good service reputation are needed to screen.

If you stay in the Navy long enough, there is a good chance you will be ordered to serve on one of the Navy's many personnel boards: augmentation (into the regular Navy), screening, promotion, decorations and awards, discharge review, aviator disposition, correction of naval records, and so on. It is an important duty, and if my experience is any guide, you will look back on such an assignment with a new respect for the diligence and integrity of those who serve on these boards. In my years of service on such boards, I can remember only one instance where there was a hint of favoritism shown, and that involved a possible bias toward one warfare community, not for or against a specific individual whose record was before the board.

20

Advice for Midshipmen

I can imagine no more rewarding a career. And any man who may be asked in this century what he did to make his life worthwhile, I think can respond with a good deal of pride and satisfaction: I served in the United States Navy.

—President John F. Kennedy, August 1, 1963, to the Naval Academy plebe class of 1967

This chapter contains some additional career advice for midshipmen and other officer candidates. Some readers will have no intention of making the Navy a career. They want to serve their country, but at some point early in their naval service they plan to return to civilian life. Still, while in service, most want to perform as well as they can and be able to look back on their naval career, however brief, as President Kennedy did. They want their time to be well spent and to learn habits of performance that will stand them well in any future endeavor.

Good advice to all regardless of career intentions is to get into the habit of performing well in any job you are assigned. We are creatures of habit, and if we try to do well and expect it of ourselves, we will continue to do it regardless of our occupation. Some young officers make a mental reservation that it is not important whether they do well. All they have to do is get by, and then when they return to the "real world," they will take things more seriously. Such thinking is wrong. You need to get into the *habit* of success; shifting paradigms is not easy, and success is not assured.

It is never too early to start to gain a good professional reputation and to get into the habit of success. You Naval Academy midshipmen in particular are already embarked on making a service reputation that will see you through a full naval career. Your fellow midshipmen will quickly size you up and will duly note improvements and declines in performance over your four years at the academy. There are seven year groups—three ahead of you and three behind your class—that will march through a naval career with most of you. Accordingly, for good or ill you already are gaining a solid basis for a service reputation.

For officers from commissioning sources other than the academy, your service reputation base starts out narrower because you have fewer midshipmen in your NROTC unit or fewer officer candidates in your class. But this disadvantage starts declining when you enter the fleet, and before too long you have caught up to your academy peers.

When I was commandant of midshipmen at the academy, I was struck by the eagerness of midshipmen to find out what it was like in the "real Navy" and to get practical advice they could put to immediate use. They did not want long lists of sterling qualities that were the sought-for objectives; they wanted to know *how* to do it: how to be a success as a junior officer and ultimately become a senior officer in command.

Some years ago a senior officer addressed the junior class at the academy as a group and gave them career advice. The advice was in the form of ten commandments and is applicable to all candidates for a commission.

1. *Go where the action is.* With regard to service selection, the senior officer's advice was the Navy equivalent to the Army's "marching to the sound of guns." Try to get a ship that is going to war. In peacetime select a ship that will soon be a deployer. Get into the combat forces and not support occupations. This advice was not intended to offend those going into the restricted line or staff corps (some of them go

to war, too), but to tell midshipmen that our service is a war-fighting one and that success is largely determined by how good you prepare as a war fighter. You cannot always predict when a war will occur or when the action will start to heat up, but you can play the odds and go where you think the action will be.

2. *Seek to work for the best officers you can find.* This is another variable over which you do not have a great deal of control. Nevertheless, you may be surprised to find that even in an era of long training pipelines, you often have some say over what department or subunit you are assigned to—perhaps not right after reporting aboard but later when you get your sea legs. Do not be afraid to work for "sundowners" or "iron pants" or "hard but fair" leaders. They will teach you the seagoing profession.

3. *Prepare yourself for command.* If you have read the earlier chapters of this book, you do not need any further elaboration on this point.

4. *Be the first to get qualified.* As a junior officer in any unit, you will face a succession of qualification hurdles—to get your dolphins, your surface war officer (SWO) pin, your plane commander designation, your chief engineer qualification, your department head qualification, and so on. All such qualifications take a great deal of study that you must do on your own. Look for a division officer or junior division officer billet to get early experience in leading Sailors. By the way, leading Sailors is more rewarding and more fun than leading your classmates at the academy, your NROTC unit, or OCS.

5. *Look for opportunities to educate yourself.* Your education should not stop when you get your academy or college diploma. Your professional growth will depend greatly on your ability to study on your own, to observe keenly what is going on around you, to mentally "fleet up," and to cultivate what aviators call "situational awareness." Take correspondence courses to keep your intellectual tool locker energized.

6. *Do not rest on your Naval Academy background.* Bear in mind that the senior officer was speaking to Naval Academy juniors. There is a

tendency among some academy midshipmen to believe that their academy background will carry them through their early career and that extra effort is not required. The academy staff works hard to overcome that misperception. This principle applies to whatever your background. If you have prior enlisted service and graduate from OCS, you cannot rest on your prior fleet service as giving you a head start for long.

7. *Do not worry who gets the credit.* You may run into shipmates—perhaps even some bosses—who will take the credit when things go right. Do not worry about it; the people who count will know where the truth lies, and your reputation will be enhanced if you do not jostle for the limelight.

8. *Stay as close to the operating forces as you can.* This is still good counsel for junior officers but must be tempered when applied to more-senior officers. For example, senior officers cannot afford to spend more time on fleet staffs (even deploying fleet staffs) if they need a responsible job in Washington to round out their career or to prepare for such a job in a prior apprenticeship tour.

9. *Keep your sense of humor.* A naval career can be, and indeed should be, fun. Part of the makeup of most successful officers is a keen sense of humor. This is not the ability to laugh at the foibles of others but at oneself. A sense of humor adds to your perspective of proportion and balance, makes you a better shipmate, and eases you over the inevitable disappointments of a Navy career.

10. *Take all career advice (including this) with a grain of salt.* There are many roads to career success, and many think theirs is the only sure one. As a junior officer you will receive much advice. Take it seriously, but consider it in the context of the speaker's situation and other advice you receive.

I would add two more "commandments":

11. *Look out for your men and women*—but that is only half of the bargain. The other half is that they must measure up to your standards.

Too many junior officers construe the first half to mean blind support for their enlisted personnel at mast, special request chits, and so on, without insisting on their performing at a level that warrants your loyalty. Your job as a leader is to set the terms of the bargain and see that the bargain is kept. Loyalty is a two-way street. One of the marks of professional officers is that they are mission oriented.

12. *You will succeed or fail as a division officer, department head, or skipper depending on your relationship with your chief petty officers.* Cultivating a positive relationship with them, one that puts the unit first, is your most important job aside from developing competence in operating your weapons system.

Although it is not advice, you might benefit from an observation I heard from my company officer while I was a plebe at the academy. In a gathering of plebes in my company, he noted: "What it takes to make a success of a naval career is a high resistance to frustration." Frequently you will be frustrated because you are not calling the shots. You seldom do in any career—particularly as a junior officer or junior executive.[1] You must learn to handle it by using your mind rather than your emotions to guide you through the rough spots. One technique already mentioned is to rehearse in your own mind how you would do things differently if you were the skipper (or that individual's boss!).

A delusion held by some midshipmen and officer candidates is that things will be different when they get in the *real* Navy (and away from the military Mickey Mouse where they are now). Some midshipmen believe they are already junior officers and should be treated as such. And some of the people running the Navy's officer programs perpetuate that misconception by telling their charges that they *are* junior officers—and should start acting like it. Many midshipmen hear the first part of the sentence and forget the rest. Any commissioning program requires rules and regulations designed to make students qualified to receive a commission. Some rules are better than others, but together they compose a complete set. They change over time with circumstances in the service and in society, but to complain about them while you are in the process is to set a bad precedent for yourself (complaining is a carryover sport).

When you graduate from the program, your perspective will change. Let me take some time here for another sea story. The rigors of plebe year at the Naval Academy change over time, but most of those who have been through it are proud of the experience and are reluctant to see the program changed. A former commandant of midshipmen (not me), when addressing the plebe class as a group, posed this question to them: "Suppose I were to propose that we drop the rigors of plebe year—no more running to formation, no more compulsory knowledge rules, no more rigorous bracing up . . ." The cheers were deafening. Then he dropped the clincher: " . . . *but only after the end of the current plebe year!*" The groans were similarly deafening. Any rite of passage takes on a special aura with the passage of time.

Speaking of rites of passage, one in most Navy commissioning programs is what is called "service selection" or, in the case of aviation officer candidate programs, "pipeline selection" (what types of aircraft you will be trained to fly). Sometimes the structure of the program or process, your professional grades in training, or pure luck makes the decision for you. But if you do have a choice, your selection can be extremely important to your future career and how well you do in it. It deserves careful thought. Too many fledgling officers make the choice for superficial reasons, as a result of peer pressure as to what is considered glamorous, or because assignment to a particular locale appears attractive. In a recent article in an Annapolis newspaper, a midshipman was interviewed about his career choice. His response was that he was selecting a duty station near his girlfriend's home but hated to give up the chance for duty in Hawaii. Others (if they can) select a staff corps or restricted line option "because I didn't enjoy going to sea on my summer cruises." These snapshots should tell you how *not* to service select. For those of you who plan to go into special warfare (become SEALs), I will caution you that it is a young man's specialty. You cannot fly or be a SEAL for an entire Navy career. By the time you are a senior lieutenant commander, most of your flying or being underwater will be behind you.

Similarly in patrol aviation—an important professional specialty—you will find that most of your duty will not involve going to sea or, in many cases, close contact with other fleet units. Almost all of your career will be spent based ashore. That may suit you just fine, but it does shut down some full career options and prospects. My advice to those of you who aspire to serve in the proud ranks of patrol aviation: take every opportunity to serve with forces afloat.[2] The focus of a Sailor's career is the sea, not just flying over or sailing under it. Your watchwords in service selection should be: sea, combat, and early responsibility.

I will offer one final piece of advice here. In the fleet, you will be serving with officers from many commissioning sources—the Naval Academy, NROTC, OCS, warrant officers, and LDOs up from the enlisted ranks. The sharp edges that are so evident to midshipmen and junior officers blur over time, and you will soon not give the commissioning source of your associates a second thought as they become shipmates and friends, colleagues, bosses, and subordinates. You will find that what counts is not a commissioning source but how well the officer performs—whether the individual is a professional. You will also find that you must compete on your own merits and that over the long run you have no built-in advantage over your running mates. You must get that advantage the old-fashioned way: you must earn it.

21

Advice for Those
Who Have Missed a Hurdle

All advice is opinion.
—Anonymous

What if you were not on the screening or promotion selection list? For most it is a crushing blow because it is unexpected. You received what you considered were good, solid fitness reports and touched most if not all the career development bases. You may have had a stumble early in your career but thought you had put it behind you. Or you tried hard to get the really good jobs, but something always seemed to get in the way of a desired assignment. But what really got you were the numbers. Statistically, it is impossible for all good and qualified officers to make the grade of commander and captain, to say nothing of flag. That is not to say your services are not needed. Many important billets need to be filled, and you are qualified to fill many of them. Unfortunately for you, it is not likely that you will be asked to fill those billets at the more senior grades.

When I was a plebe at the Naval Academy, a commissioned officer on the staff told a group of us: "If you make commander in the Navy, you have had a good solid career. If you make captain you have been very successful. And if you make flag you are not only good but lucky."[1] If you have failed of selection for the first time, you have a major decision to make. You can take any one of three paths: you can resign or retire if eligible, you can seek billets in the near term that are more personally satisfying as you look ahead to a second career in civilian life, or you can seek a billet that may improve your chances of selection the next time around.

Weighing the Decision to Stay or Go

Almost every promotion board picks some officers from *above* the promotion zone, that is, from the pool of officers who have been passed over one or more times. Boards stick with this practice even at the price of denying selection to an officer in the promotion zone. There is a widespread conviction that an incentive must be provided for the very best officers previously overlooked for promotion. For the passed-over officer, it is a very difficult decision to stay on the career track for one more turn before the next board. It does not help that keen disappointment clouds one's judgment at such a time. But bear in mind that the next board will be made up of officers who did not serve on your last board.

What should you do? If you have found out informally that you were close to the cusp for selection, or if you believe that is the case, it could be wise to take another turn before the next board.[2] If you are due for orders, talk to your detailer and get that individual's advice as to what assignments on offer might push you over the top. On the other hand, if accepting such an assignment would lock you into a longer tour than you are willing to risk, you should look around for a tour that better fits in with your future plans—perhaps to a location you want or a job experience that would fill out your job search resume.

Plenty of satisfying jobs are available for officers who have failed of selection. After all, you have the experience; you just lack the rank. Shrewd placement officers and commanding officers of some commands know what a treasure trove lies in the pool of officers who have been passed over. In that pool are some officers who have held command, many of them successful in their command tours. There are officers whose resume perhaps was unbalanced by too much shore duty but have just the experience needed for another demanding and satisfying shore tour. With few exceptions the pool contains officers who would be instantly recalled in the event of war or a major national emergency.

If you are being considered for a desirable job that may just put you over the top, you might want to campaign for the job by visiting the skipper of that command and impressing on that individual your credentials and continued desire to compete. But overhanging these options and decisions is the fact that you are getting nearer to having to start your second career. Everyone in the Navy has to think sooner or later about such a career. If you are a passed-over officer, that decision is coming sooner, but it was inevitable in any case. You begin to realize that the Navy is a young man's or woman's service, and you have to consider when you want to start your second career. Often, but not always, sooner is better than later—particularly if you have family obligations.

I will give some advice here: do not go into automatic if you get the bad news. Do not head for the door right away—particularly when your disappointment is high. Give the decision to go or stay the same deep thought that you have given each step of your career to this point. Do not too quickly reject the option of giving it another try. You are still a good officer. You still have a good future inside or outside the Navy. The question is always what it has been from the beginning: a matter of timing and careful decision making.

Most officers who fail of selection are disappointed but accept that disappointment with good grace and a mature acceptance of responsibility for the success of their naval career. But you will also hear some explanations and complaints, and we should examine them. This listing of oft-heard complaints is not intended to mock officers who have been passed over or failed to screen. Rather, it is intended to provide a sampling of warning signals for you to heed as you chart your own career before you are confronted with a career disappointment.

Frequently Heard Explanations

Many excuses have as their basis a failure to accept responsibility for one's own actions and a willingness to place blame elsewhere.

1. *"I was set up to fail."* The speaker goes on to say, "I was given an impossible job (or given no support from my seniors), so I was the scapegoat." This lament parallels what I consider one of the most whining paragraphs in modern literature: "More and more it was beginning to appear that he had been asked to do the impossible, but if he failed it would not be remembered that he had been asked to do the impossible. It would only be remembered that he had failed."[3]

   The Marine recruiting poster puts it well: "No one promised you a rose garden." Many if not most jobs in the Navy are very demanding. Few are impossible. There are challenges to be overcome and a few windmills around to tilt at. But I have never seen anyone be set up to fail—with one possible exception. In the early 1970s, when the Navy had a major recruiting and retention crisis, some ships were very low in qualified engineering personnel. Most skippers did their best to get through the crisis—asking their commodores to borrow personnel from nondeployers, bootstrapping their nonrated personnel to qualify them, cutting back to only two steaming watch sections, and asking for other help. The Navy was stretched thin, and part of it finally broke: one oiler skipper with his back to the wall refused to sail and placed his ship in C-4 status because of an insufficient number of qualified engineering personnel. This action reverberated throughout the Navy, and most praised the courage and integrity of the skipper. But his superiors should have taken on this decision before he had to. He put his career on the line because his conscience told him he had to. This story is so well known because it is not typical. Few officers are set up to fail or denied the resources to do the job. And even then there is a way out if they have the courage we expect of our officers.

2. *"My skipper had it in for me."* When you hear this explanation, your first questions should be: Why was that? What is it about you that ticked that person off? Did the skipper have it in for others, too? Commanding officers did not get to where they are by randomly picking on subordinates. Some subordinates require more attention or supervision than others. One recalls the legendary fitness report quip: "I would trust this officer with my wife, but not with my ship." Repeated subpar performance calls for increased supervision that in turn can be interpreted as harassment by the poor performer. In extreme cases a diligent skipper follows Admiral Benitez's maxim: "If a subordinate repeatedly fails to measure up despite continuous counseling, act decisively. Relieve that person from his or her duties, no matter how painful the experience."[4] Being relieved is a one-way ticket to a failure of selection in almost every case. It should come as no surprise that officers who are relieved usually believe they have been injured unfairly.

   Some skippers are more patient than others. And some are more decisive than others. Still others work around the problem, and the poor performers soon find themselves ignored and their work being done by others. You try a skipper's patience at your professional peril, and if you find others attempting to do your job, you are receiving an early warning of the need to improve your performance.

3. *"I can't understand why I wasn't selected—I had good jobs and did them well."* A detailer's typical "day after" phone call with a disappointed constituent whose weak record fell out during the first round might go something like this:

OFFICER: I got the word that I didn't screen for command. I've got a great record—all my former COs said I was a shoe-in. What happened?

DETAILER: I'm sorry, Jim, but you didn't make it. Let's talk about where you go from here. You'll get your last look next year.

OFFICER: You know, I can't say who it was, but one of my mentors was on the board. He said that I crunched five times and fell out at the last vote.

DETAILER: Jim, I'm not really at liberty to discuss board deliberations. But I'd guess that your lack of breakouts as a department head and two tours in low-impact shore jobs didn't help you. You turned down a great operational ride to take your job in the N4 shop at COMSHORELANT, but I've got a great billet opening up on the Seventh Fleet staff in six months. Are you interested?

OFFICER: What do you have available in Boston?

4. *"My skipper was interested only in his own future."* The listener should pose the question, "What is the connection with your failure to be selected?" It is easy to confuse an appropriate zeal to meet the command's mission and advance its performance and welfare with the skipper's self-interest. By definition the skipper is the only person with total responsibility for the command. It is true that some skippers confuse command performance with personal advancement. Still, to suggest that is the skipper's primary focus is to attribute base motives to that individual and by implication better motives to the speaker.

   In a worst-case situation, that leaves the unanswered question of how the allegation of self-interest is connected to a subordinate's failure to be selected for promotion. Your skipper wants to see you promoted if you deserve it. Even the most self-interested and self-promoting skipper has an interest in seeing you perform well and being promoted if that performance justifies it. It is not a zero-sum game. If you hear this excuse, you are face to face with the reason the complaining officer was not promoted.

5. *"I tried to get good assignments, but the detailer dealt me a bad hand."* Your assignment officer deals in a market of matching people to billets and trying to make you and your prospective commanding officer happy. Most officers in the marketplace are seeking the most professionally enhancing assignments, that is, assignments that if performed well give the incumbent a leg up before future screening

and promotion boards. Many are called and few are chosen for the plum assignments. It is a simple matter of arithmetic.

At the lieutenant and lieutenant commander level, those desired assignments are as department heads in ships or squadrons. The detailer, the placement officer (who represents your future commanding officer), and your future skipper want the best match of skills for those important and desirable jobs—and they want the best performers in them.

Detailers have a good sense of the quality of your performance record. To help them understand that record, they have a rough summary grade as to where you stand in the talent pool. Their boss is looking over their shoulder to see that the best go to the best (i.e., most demanding and therefore most desirable) jobs. Detailers who play favorites do not last very long. So when you hear the excuse that someone was mishandled by the detailer, it means in most cases that the speaker's record simply was not strong enough to make the cut for the best jobs.

The unstated backdrop of this excuse is that officers who express this complaint had an inflated opinion of their performance relative to that of their peers and competitors. It is easy to fall into this trap because commanding officers write good fitness reports if an officer is at least satisfactory. Reading such reports, naïve also-rans can come to the self-flattering conclusion that they are competitors and have broken out of the pack even if the recommended promotion section of the fitness report suggests otherwise. But in the marketplace it is comparative performance that counts. That is why it is a good idea to review your jacket. Better yet, get a senior friend to go over your record with you and get some sense as to how you stack up.

As you go over your record, fitness report after fitness report to note how you stack up, read the numbers in the promotion recommendation section as well as the words. Did your skipper indicate that you are qualified for the next step up the promotion ladder? If not, and you are still aboard, you need to get that individual to counsel you on what you need to do to get that qualification.

6. *"My ship (or squadron) was cliquish; you were either on the boss's team or you were not."* The speaker is by self-definition an outsider. There are "horizontal cliques," that is, cliques or groups made up of peers who happen to like each other's company. It is nothing different from the social selection that goes on in all parts of any society, including the schools we attended before entering the service. Although the value of being a member of such groups is overrated, and the payoff is mostly in increased self-esteem, there is an understandable disappointment in not being included. But such exclusion rarely damages an otherwise good officer's promotion prospects.

"Vertical cliques," where they exist, can be more damaging to the command and the individual who is not a member. A vertical clique is a group that crosses major seniority boundaries. The basis for group cohesion may be social, regional, or, in rare cases, commissioning source background. Such vertical cliques are credibly viewed as a system of favoritism. I confess that although I have seen such cliques in civilian life, I have not seen them in a ship wardroom or squadron ready room. The officer who perceives a vertical clique may instead be seeing a group of top or (more rarely) bottom performers who seek some form of kinship and ease of interaction with like-minded individuals. I have never met a skipper or XO who would foster such an atmosphere. Their self-interest dictates inclusiveness.

7. *"I made a single mistake, and it did me in."* This is a rare admission. The statement may well be true, but the mistake may not have been a small one. And in a competition of the best, when the call may be close, one mistake may be one too many. It is a tough world, and in the Navy it is meant to be tough because people's lives are at stake.

Usually, a mistake made as a junior officer is more easily and rapidly put aside than one made at a more senior grade, where the selection screen gets much finer. I have known flag officers who made mistakes when they were junior officers and rose to outlive them. It is more difficult to overcome similar mistakes in the grade of commander and captain, but in some cases officers have had so much potential to offer the Navy that their career has been saved to realize that promise.

In the era when groundings or brush collisions at sea were much more common than they are today, there was much chortling in the ranks when some good skipper ("water walker, shoe-in for flag") crossed the boundaries between good seamanship and risking his ship. Some of these gentlemen were war heroes and given another chance. Yes, there was some luck involved and maybe some favoritism from high places. But as I view these cases, I can think of only one that was not justified by the subsequent distinguished career of the officer who faltered.

8. *"My spouse wanted me to accept a shore assignment."* Blaming the spouse or pointing to conflicting family obligations that take the speaker off the career track are prima facie evidence of a self-imposed (perhaps with the best of reasons) limit on promotability. The reasons may be valid enough, but there are enough other candidates for promotion without such problems that the Navy picks its future leadership from their number.

9. *"I was unlucky."* Luck plays some part in every career, but my experience tells me that it is seldom the decisive factor. Admiral Benitez reminds us: "There is an unexplainable sequence in life with mysteries that defy rational explanation. Don't waste time lamenting the capriciousness of the unexplainable."[5]

At the extreme, bad luck (events beyond your control to avoid or prepare for) can be decisive, but much more often it is not. Most of what passes for good luck is meticulous preparation for the unexpected and the unknowable. You must be prepared to accept responsibility for bad luck as well as good fortune. If bad luck dogs your career and good fortune always seems to go to your competitors in the race, you need to look within to change things.

There is a rule in football that makes the officials part of the playing field. That is, if the official gets in the way of the play, he should be considered as part of the turf and its dimensions. It is useless to complain about circumstances that place him in your path. It is your job to avoid him and compensate for his presence. So it is with purported "bad luck." Do not complain about it; avoid it and think ahead to ensure it does not play a dominant role in your career.

A common theme in all these explanations and complaints is that it was somebody else's fault that you failed of selection. Blame placing is not a desirable attribute of future commanders. On the other hand, there are excuses that one rarely hears. When you do hear them, you are being reminded of the markers that define the channel you must navigate.

Rarely Heard Explanations and Complaints

1. *"It took me a while to get my stuff together."* This officer was a slow starter, and a fast finish cannot make up for some disadvantages. The race most often goes to those who both start and finish fast.

2. *"I relied on my Naval Academy education and coasted for too long."* Some Naval Academy graduates mistake a good grounding in the naval profession as sufficient to ease their promotion path to command. This is a variant of the slow-starter excuse mentioned above.

3. *"My marriage was going bad, and I was distracted."* The reader will not get any lectures here about marrying too early or on spouse selection—particularly about a prospective spouse little interested in the sacrifices called for by the naval service. Suffice it to say a marriage that is cross threaded with your career is a great disadvantage as you try to advance in your profession. You may have to choose between the two, and the process can be exceedingly painful not only to your marriage but also to your future prospects in the Navy. This is something to bear in mind when you choose your spouse—and that individual chooses you: You may be deciding not just on your life partner but on your career and your success in it as well.

4. *"I was running with a bunch of superstars."* The implication is that come fitness report time these superstars got the best fitness reports in a very competitive environment. I would observe: welcome to your future in the Navy. As you get more senior, you are *always* running with superstars, officers who have screened through a very competitive selection process. In some ways having tough competition as a junior officer is the best thing that can happen to you. First, it forces you to be on your professional toes and perform at a higher level. Second, you can learn from them. And, finally, as they (and you) progress through your careers together, you have an opportunity to foster strong friendships with the future leaders of the Navy.

5. *"I mistook my skipper's efforts in counseling as harassment."* Rarely will a skipper, executive officer, or department head not make the effort to straighten you out and point out shortcomings in your performance. They will go further and give you a program for getting back on the right track. This is not harassment. But they are not social workers. *You* must sense when you are entering shoal water by asking the right questions, reviewing your record, taking your performance and received guidance seriously, and resisting the comfortable and smug feeling that you are on the right track. Above all, you must resist the notion that the world is out of step and you are not.

6. *"I had my chance and muffed it."* Your opportunities come in many forms—and sometimes they are deeply buried behind a seabag full of problems. It is often easier to push the problems aside and look for the opportunities.[6] Opportunities have two overriding attributes: they are wrapped in hard work needed to solve problems, and they involve the risk inherent in making important decisions that can decide your career. If there is one lesson I have learned in the service, it is that there is no golden road to good performance and advancement in your naval career. The channel is littered with wrecks on either side that identify careers that lacked hard work, innate ability, or decisiveness.

22

Some Parting Shots

What greater satisfaction is there in life than in bringing your ship safely into a snug harbor after an arduous voyage when it seemed the elements conspired against you and you bore the responsibility for the ultimate outcome?

—Anonymous retired officer

In the movie *Forrest Gump,* Forrest's mother's memorable line went something like this: "Life is like a box of chocolates; you never know what you're going to get." Like much humor, there is considerable truth in that observation on choices.

A Philosophy to Live and Serve By

One's life is defined by choices (e.g., to marry or not) and imperatives over which one has no control (e.g., inherited genes). Much of the point of life is to expand one's choices to provide sufficient scope to live a useful and satisfying life. For many of us, our choices include selecting a college or university to attend, deciding on an academic major, choosing an occupation, selecting immediate or deferred payoffs, proposing marriage, deciding whether to have a child, deciding when to change jobs or retire, and so on.

Having a choice is a necessary but insufficient condition for living a useful and satisfying life. One must make good choices. But even good choices are insufficient. One must also invest the effort needed to realize the decisions made. This trilogy of strategies, that is, maximizing the scope of choice, making the right choice, and then working to realize the benefits of the path taken, applies to success in the naval profession. There are pitfalls at each decision point. Some officers limit their choices too early in their careers, others make what will be the wrong choices because of insufficient information or stubborn adherence to the preference of the moment, and still others do not apply themselves to pursuing the benefits of the correct (for them) choice. As one of the quotes at the beginning of this book said: "We may give you advice, but we cannot inspire conduct."

The two most significant obstacles to optimizing choices and to professional advancement are lack of self-knowledge and impetuosity. These hazards are particularly salient to the officer candidate and junior officer. The transient glamour or immediate financial rewards of a warfare specialty or the attractions of a particular homeport can turn the novice's head when that individual should be taking the longer view. Even as a midshipman your own predilections and circumstances are conspiring to limit your future choices, choices that will affect you for a lifetime. You may be drawn to aviation or SEAL training—or the Judge Advocate General's (JAG) Corps—by glamorous portrayals on TV or in a popular film of the moment. But you may know in your heart that you do not have the hand-eye coordination, temperament, physical stamina, or penchant for diligent study to perform well in one of these or other specialties.

It became apparent to me while I was going through flight training that some of my flight training classmates were unsuited for a career in naval aviation—and that they knew it once they started the training. In some cases it should have been apparent to them before they applied. So, they started their careers with failure as a result of impetuosity or lack of self-knowledge. Some transferred to other specialties, some were killed in training accidents, and the remainder muddled through to get their wings but had unsatisfying or short careers. The point here is that deliberation, knowing yourself, and honestly confronting your capabilities and motivations are the best investment you will ever make in life and in a naval career. This self-knowledge cannot come soon enough—and in the best of circumstances should occur before you put on the uniform.

Part of this self-knowledge is to gauge your willingness to bear the costs. The reasons for a lack of success in a naval career are many. Some misunderstood the degree of personal sacrifice entailed in a successful career. Some were lazy and did not overcome the inertia of taking the easy path. Still others fooled themselves into thinking they would do all right once they got the right job or the right boss. Others entered into a wrong marriage and saw it destroy their career prospects. And a few were unlucky. But very few were unlucky for an entire career. It is not enough to want to be a captain or flag officer; you must be willing to pay the personal price that such a promotion entails. That price includes self-denial, hard work, taking charge of your own life, and accepting responsibility for what happens along the way.

Such advice is easily said, but hard to do. What are the warning signs of potential failure?

1. Going with the flow—letting stronger people take charge of your life
2. Leaving the hard work to others or believing that such work has no payoff; believing there is an easier way or that there are workable short-cuts for smarter people (like you)
3. Making excuses for failure rather than accepting personal responsi-bility; blaming others (spouse, skipper) for your shortcomings and disappointments
4. Enjoying it now rather than later
5. Failing to gauge your own potential and limitations before being forced to
6. Gradually falling into the "loser" mode—unpaid bills, marital problems, mediocre fitness reports, gaining weight—and looking for escape mechanisms such as resignation and job change, early

retirement, extramarital affairs, divorce, bankruptcy, or blaming someone else

What are the signs of potential success?

1. A fierce and uncompromising acceptance of responsibility for your own shortcomings and for discharging your obligations to others
2. A "do it now!" mind-set
3. An ability to deny yourself the easy path, the slick solution, the luxury of a cutting corners, getting the benefit now and paying the price later (or getting someone else to pay the price for you)
4. An ability to do what you must do but hate to do—but doing it well anyway (a good piece of advice from my Naval Academy classmate Adm. Kinnaird McKee)
5. An ability to put mission first, your people second, and yourself last
6. An ability to confront the problems of life and service honestly and unemotionally build solutions that work

In the modern trendy world there is a new expert: the "life coach." These individuals help (for a sizeable fee) the wealthy and powerful organize their lives because their clients have neither the time nor the skills to do it for themselves. They provide tools of discipline to their clients by helping them organize their free time (e.g., schedule time with family for Saturday from two to four in the afternoon), their personal finances, their personal entertaining, their fitness regimen, and their workload (real or perceived) and by arranging specialized counseling when needed. Although most of us would snicker at the apparent preciousness and pretentiousness of such a concept, the fact is that most of us must undertake these functions on our own—and sometimes we do not do them very well. For better or worse, most of us must perform the duties as our own life coach. We can learn from the life coach concept by standing back and looking as objectively as we can at how we are performing. Put on your own life coach hat occasionally and examine yourself critically but constructively. What is out of balance in your life? Where do you need to improve? Where do you need help? This self-counseling can be refreshing if it is honest and tough enough.

Where Is the Fun in the Naval Profession?

You will often hear the bromide, "If you aren't having fun, you aren't doing it right." Most of the prescriptions for self-improvement in this book require hard work, attention to detail, and a tenacious devotion to duty. To some this will not sound like fun. But the "fun" in the naval profession comes from the satisfaction of a job well done, making a contribution that makes a difference, and the comradeship of those who, like yourself, like challenges, like to be tested and found up to the mark, and see the humorous side of Navy life. It is fun to serve with people you respect, with whom you have suffered hardships and experienced danger, and who appreciate your contribution to the unit, the mission, the service, and the nation.

There is an analogy in athletics. Much of any sport is hard work and dedication. But most athletes pay the price, enjoy the competition, and cherish the high of winning. You do not have to be an athlete to be a good naval officer. You can get the same elation by solving problems, guiding others to achieve a common objective, and outsmarting a capable enemy. Successful naval officers, whether athletes or not, do not experience fun through self-indulgence, "good times," or ego trips. Rather, they enjoy being part of a team with an objective higher than themselves, overcoming adversity, and being part of a band of brothers and sisters who have met the test of courage, honor, and commitment.

Taking the Long View

In this book we have taken a cruise together through the Navy's assignment and promotion systems, and the time has come to say good-bye. I have left much out of the log of this journey—such as the paramount importance of personal integrity, the need for courage in the face of adversity, and the importance of preparing yourself to handle the stress of the long watches and the demands of duty when it would be easier to fall into bed and let someone else worry about things. I have emphasized the importance of performance, hard work, situational awareness, and the sensors that will keep us out of shoal water.

My seaman's eye tells me that most of the officers I served with were capable of making flag. Many wanted to return to civilian life early in their naval careers. Others were unwilling or unable to make the sacrifices that would have been required to reach the top of their profession. Many others were proud and able Sailors but fell to the numbers attrition exacted at each promotion point. The point is that if you get your commission, advancement to the top of your profession is within your reach. Whether it is in your grasp is largely up to you—not some impersonal system that devours its own and not some crap game contingent on the roll of the dice. This judgment will not be popular with some readers who see the opponent as an impersonal system programmed to frustrate them at every turn. My counsel to those who believe that comfortable judgment is that life will be difficult for you in or outside the service. The service has merely held you accountable more quickly than you like.

One of the characteristics of successful naval officers (of whatever rank) that I find most appealing and warranting of respect is their fearless acceptance of responsibility. Most do not whine, make excuses, or look for scapegoats. They realize that their profession is a hard one that requires personal commitment, courage, and integrity and that the risks to themselves and to their unit can be very high. But they are not reckless risk takers. They take risks when the stakes are high enough and the odds give them a chance to succeed. They ask nothing more. One of the intangible benefits of naval service is that people of this type surround you: they lead you, they follow you, and they give you a hand when you offer it. No man or woman can ask for more.

The naval profession is one long love affair. There are bumps and valleys but there are also indescribable highs. There are parts of your career that you would just as soon forget: the chewing out that you received—and richly deserved, the near miss with another ship or a nearby shoal, the frequent reminders that you are not as good as you think you are, the gradual understanding that you depended on others more than they depended on you, and your first time in combat and the nagging question of whether you would measure up. But there are other parts you will never forget: the "well done" from a respected senior for a job completed in the face of great difficulties; the glory of homecoming after a long, arduous, and successful deployment; the sense of comradeship with your fellow Sailors and aviators; and the joy and pride on a well-deserved promotion or decoration and the attendant knowledge that you had measured up. This glow will follow you into retirement. There is no more emotional event outside of marriage that compares to a reunion with old shipmates, with the reliving of shared experience, hardship, and danger. They are living testimony that you served well and with a band of heroes. No one can take that experience away from you. Indeed, those who have not served will not even understand it. But you will, and your shipmates will. What you are experiencing is the joyful song of a grateful nation saying thank you.

Appendix A

Dilemmas and Paradoxes in a Naval Career

Much of the material in this appendix has already been covered in a different form in the body of this book. Still, some elaboration might be useful, focusing on specific dilemmas that are likely to be faced in a naval career. Look on this material as a group of extended footnotes placed here to avoid cluttering up the text. To some, these dilemmas are more imaginary than real. Some see life as a simple series of choices to be selected from rationally—a misleading caricature of the philosophy laid out in the last chapter. That extreme perspective gives short shrift to officers who do not see things in black-and-white terms and have healthy doubts about their ability to select achievable goals and the competence to navigate a safe course through the many hazards.

Therefore, this appendix is for officers who reflect on their situation and not for officers who are never afflicted with self-doubts. Few recommendations are offered in the discussion that follows. The key part of problem solving is the articulation and structuring of the problem. When that is in hand, solutions often supply themselves. It helps to think about problems in advance so that we recognize them when they appear and have already done some intellectual spadework in preparing for them.

Loyalty versus Integrity

Some will assert that there is no dilemma, that a loyal officer is an officer with integrity and vice versa. We should not conclude that too quickly, however. Although loyalty to an institution such as the Navy might partially coincide with integrity, loyalty to a person (e.g., a senior or classmate) can conflict with integrity as it applies to an institution. This dilemma can occur as early as midshipman days when one is tempted or asked to cover for or "not bilge" a classmate or teammate. One of the realities of academy and college life is a fierce loyalty to contemporaries: classmates, fraternity brothers or sorority sisters, teammates, and company mates. Loyalty to persons is an integral part of daily life, and the institution, although important, is seen as "them" and not "us." The honor systems of the service academies sometimes founder on this dilemma because the integrity ethos is so foreign to much of our upbringing and natural inclinations. Loyalty is relatively easy, and integrity is often difficult and exacts consequences. If you have not already faced this dilemma as a midshipman or officer candidate, you will at some point in your career as a naval officer.

When a choice is posed between loyalty and integrity, it means the system's integrity is breaking down. The danger in loyalty is that it is too often diverted to a person or an office rather than the institution that the person or office serves. But it is the person or office one encounters daily, not the largely faceless institution. One does not form friendships and personal bonds with institutions, but with real people. They are classmates, shipmates, imperfect bosses, and subordinates. One learns to love, respect, and cherish them (or most of them), but those feelings must end when duty is encountered. That is the hard decision facing officers who would do their duty. Seniors in particular must not impose the need for choice either knowingly or unknowingly on subordinates.

Still, loyalty—consistent with one's duty—to one's commanding officer and one's shipmates is what holds the institution together. The answer is to be loyal right up to the point where integrity is compromised. All the societal pressures of the naval service argue for carrying loyalty over to the domain of integrity. The best naval officers resist that pressure even at the risk of destruction of their careers and lives. The only consolation in all this is that anything worthwhile demands a high price. It is demeaning to attempt to do what is right and then whine about the price to be paid.

Family versus Service

In most cases this dilemma is slow to emerge, but with the passage of years and the presence of a growing family, it becomes more salient to the serious naval officer. Some couples see no dilemma: the service comes first, and family hardships are accepted. Such difficulties as family separations, moving to areas with substandard schools, deployments, and income that falls short of perceived needs are accepted in the name of the service.[1] At the other extreme are couples who sacrifice everything for the welfare of their children or their own creature comforts or to getting ready for an eventual return to civilian life. Most of us lie between these two poles and have to make decisions from time to time that judge the balance at that point. And the point of balance does change as the years pass.

For example, caring for a child with disabilities can lead to a fundamental decision of accepting a less career-enhancing assignment but one located where medical help is more readily available. A working spouse whose income is needed to meet anticipated college education expenses has his or her own career needs that are often in conflict with those of the Navy spouse. Painful decisions sometimes must be made. Some marriages are torn apart by these decisions. In some cases where both spouses are in the military, the problems that need to be solved can be more painful still. There is no one-size-fits-all advice for these circumstances. But there are some general guidelines that can prepare for the pain of unwanted dilemmas.

1. *Prepare.* Make every effort to discuss possible career and family conflicts before the marriage. People have a general reluctance to do this. Other things are foremost at this point in a relationship. Moreover, there is an unshakable belief that love can conquer all. No amount of prior talk will head off an unwanted decision, but prior discussion will make it easier to discuss the matter when it comes and head off recriminations that stand in the way of a good solution.
2. *Seek counseling.* I am not talking here about marriage counseling (though some may be needed), but about counseling with friends,

mentors, skippers, and parents to talk the problem through and be sure you have not overlooked some important options and factors in your decision. Your XO or skipper is a good place to start. Before entering such counseling, think through each aspect of the problem: budget impact, schools, medical care, career prospects of both spouses, and so on and lay out the costs and benefits.

3. *Do not decide in haste.* Most career dilemmas brew up over an extended period, and few require fast solutions. Turning your back on a Navy career may be the best solution for you, but once the decision is made, it is nearly irrevocable.

4. *Have a plan.* Once you decide, lay out the steps necessary to realize the decision. Indicate subsequent decision points. Adjust the plan as circumstances change.

5. *Accept the consequences of your decision.* Once you decide, there will be temptations to have second thoughts, to try to return to the decision and tinker with it to reduce its unpleasant consequences. This is a natural tendency, and its anticipated occurrence should be part of your original decision and subsequent planning. Circumstances can change, but be careful not to be blown by the latest wind or a sense of remorse.

Formal Education versus Sea Service

This dilemma may be faced both early and late in a career. Do you go for that postgraduate course, the war college tour, or a course that more firmly keeps you in competition for the next screening or promotion hurdle? Those who are more conservative and are already preparing for the eventual return to civilian life often opt for formal education. Their calculation is that more education is useful both in service and in a postservice career. They are already hedging their bets. Or perhaps they like the career path that more professional education might lead to. For example, they are attracted to an engineering duty (EDO) or aeronautical engineering duty (AEDO) career—transferring from the unrestricted line. Further formal education is needed in those and other specialties. So your decision to continue your education may have two dimensions: preparing for civilian life and preparing for a service career field that requires more formal education. Most billets requiring such education are ashore.

In earlier days (say up to the 1970s) an officer could do both. More formal education was often a career plus. When I was a junior officer it was expected that we as professional officers would attend a postgraduate course of instruction. Articles in the *Navy Times* correlated the selection opportunities of those who had attended such instruction and those who had not. The nod usually went to those who had furthered their education. The subject has become more clouded in recent years because of the extension of training pipelines for assignment to sea duty, the increase in the number of nuclear-qualified officers, and the proliferation of short and/or off-duty soft-skill master's programs.[2] The result is that today the benefits of postgraduate or war college instruction in furthering your career is more problematic. How can we structure this dilemma so as to provide some guidance for the ambitious officer? You might find the following set of questions useful.

1. What is your *principal* motive for pursuing a postgraduate course of instruction? To be a better sea officer? To be a better officer in shore billets? To get ready for a civilian career? To add to your resume? For the intellectual challenge? To prepare for a possible transfer to the restricted line or staff corps? Ordering these questions in some sort of priority and being brutally honest with yourself will tell you a great deal about your true priorities.

2. Which do you enjoy more: challenges to your intellect or challenges to your character? You must choose even if your first answer might be both.

3. Do you really enjoy going to sea, or do you consider it simply a necessary step in your career progression?

4. Is command at sea or attainment of high rank your ultimate career objective?

5. Is qualifying for a rewarding second career of major concern to you?
6. Which do you enjoy more: leading Sailors or managing resources? Also, what do you like better: tactical decision making afloat or advising top leadership on major decisions?
7. Which do you enjoy more: arguing from the abstract to the specific or from experience to general rules?

Although these questions are simplistic and limit choice, your honest answers will tell you much about yourself and the directions you might take. Bear in mind that the Navy needs postgraduate-educated officers for a large number of billets (mostly ashore). Note, though, that here we are discussing what you want to do, not what the Navy needs to staff the shore establishment. In deciding on postgraduate instruction you need to integrate the following: staying well positioned for successful sea command (if that is what you want), picking a career path that is most attuned to your skills and interests, and building an experience and intellectual base for your second career.

Short Career versus Long Career

Some would turn this dilemma into an actuarial and future income discounting problem. They would argue that if you consider both your first and second career income streams (including your Navy retired pay), you are better off financially by retiring when you are first eligible to do so. Many in this group also argue that you are better off taking an early rather than a later social security benefit. This simple formulation—particularly persuasive to career enlisted personnel—overlooks that intangible called workplace satisfaction and the largely unknowable chances of achieving higher rank.

If one were to proceed narrowly on this basis, one would aim at promotion to the rank of commander and retire at the twenty-year point before coming up before the captain promotion board. On the way you would pick up as much education at Navy expense as you could and, after selection to commander, seek jobs that enhance your civilian resume. Your last sea duty might be as a lieutenant commander on the verge of selection to commander.

This approach will appeal to some. But for others, a twenty-year commitment to a job whose only satisfaction is the prospect of early retirement would argue that you should leave even sooner—perhaps at the first release from active duty (RAD) date or after your additional obligated service for postgraduate education date.

I would offer an alternative strategy, a strategy foreshadowed in the early chapters of this book. I suggest entering the service with an initial commitment to the long-career strategy. In your early twenties you cannot be very sure of where and how you want to spend the rest of your life. Throw your hat in the long-career ring, work hard and perform well, and see how it goes. Keep your options open as long as you can. Get in the habit of doing a good job because you are committed to a long career and because it is the most valuable tool you will have—long career or short career. If things do not go well for you or you become disenchanted with the prospect of further service, you can shift gears. At the ten-year point in your career, you should have a pretty good idea of how the prospect of a long career suits you.

Comparative versus Absolute Performance

This is a dilemma of delusion—often self-delusion. You will encounter officers who throughout their careers have been advised by their bosses, mentors, and friends that they are doing an excellent job and should get over the next hurdle easily. Many of these officers will not be screened or selected for promotion not because they were not good enough but because others were better qualified or showed more promise for future development in the eyes of selection boards. Like it or not, life and a naval career are competitive. You are expected to be good—and the vast majority of officers are, but the prize goes to the *best.* One may argue that the best are not always selected, but from the very beginning the objective of selection and promotion systems is to select the best. By definition, "best" is a comparative term.

It is easy to persuade yourself that you are doing a good job and should be promoted or screened. But look around you. In looking at your fitness reports, ask yourself: Am I the best in my unit? Am I really putting out my best effort? Could it be that I am deluding myself? Am I ranked among the highest in the comparative evaluation that is part of every fitness report? The words may be nice, but the breakout is the key. Are you a "packer," or do you break out? If you do not know, your detailer can tell you.

Earlier in this book I pointed out that if you are the best, the best assignments will seek you out. If you constantly have to push the system, argue with your detailer, or campaign for a good job, you should be receiving a message. At a minimum you are not yet among the best. This is not to say that you should not take an active role in managing your career, but if you always seem to find "the system" pushing against you, you are seeing the first harbingers of career trouble.

Wait a minute, you may say. The picture you are painting is a dog-eat-dog career environment, a zero-sum game, a winner-take-all race, and I am not interested. Most career officers do not agree with such a sour appraisal. Good comparative performance is vital to screening and promotion, but your focus should be on pushing yourself, not on how your shipmate-competitors are doing. You should be focusing on doing your job well, not taking on the role of the referee at the finish line. Over a full career I have observed some very strong wardrooms and ready rooms, ones that were loaded up with superb officers. Yes, their skippers had to rank them, but most of those top-running officers did not let that fact poison their relations with each other. Most became close friends, and over time all or almost all were screened and promoted.

Some pose the dilemma: should I be a good shipmate or a strong competitor? The answer is easy: both. The strong competitor part should focus on one's own performance, not on how the others in the race are doing. There is a payoff in this attitude that goes beyond eventual screening and promotion. You will be a good shipmate, you will enjoy your tour, and if in the end you are denied the trophy, you will know that you gave it your best and can take pride in a race well run.

Appendix B

All Detailing Is Local[1]
—Comdr. Clay Harris, USN

While technically trained officers may or may not be better qualified to foster rapid and effective transformation, they will affect the process only if they are assigned to billets that offer them that opportunity.

I recently completed a tour at the Naval Personnel Command (PERS-4). I fielded many queries from senior and flag officers that wished to secure surface commanders with particular qualifications for their staffs. I did not keep a log of these transactions, but my tally would have looked like this:

- Requests for officers screened for command at sea: hundreds
    Required skills: usually unspecified and generally irrelevant
- Requests for financial managers: scores
    Required skills: addition and subtraction; high pain tolerance
- Requests for politico-military and strategy-policy specialists: dozens
    Required skills: reading and writing; high alcohol tolerance
- Requests for manpower and personnel managers: tens
    Required skills: addition and subtraction; multiplication and division (during Board sessions); plane geometry (to account for the detailing triangle); talking and listening
- Requests for logisticians: perhaps seven
    Required skills: addition and subtraction; multiplication and division; ability to read and understand shipping documents
- Requests for computer/network/C4I experts: about five
    Required skills: computer/network/C4I experience

- Requests for operations analysts: maybe four
    Required skills: multiplying and dividing; some algebra
- Requests for surface nuclear officers: around three
    Required skills: nuclear engineering

These data suggest that surface line officers with technical backgrounds are not in terribly high demand. Nor are they necessarily assigned to jobs that capitalize on their specialized talents. Current distribution priorities actively discourage detailers from assigning surface line officers to billets based on the officers' education. The exceptions tend to be joint specialty officer billets and instructor assignments, where the gaining command prizes education and training over other factors. Furthermore, our corporate perception of an officer's potential remains linked to that officer's promotion and screening status. Many staffs would rather train an upwardly mobile officer who knows little about the work at hand than accept a highly motivated subject matter expert whose record did not compete favorably at the last promotion or screening board.

Appendix C

The Junior Officer's Professional Library

You might be concerned about the thought of a personal library. You might be thinking, "When do I have time to read all that stuff? Why do I want to lug that stuff around with me? I read that kind of thing at the Naval Academy (or OCS, or at the Unit). I do not have room for it." The library cited here, however, will fit in two small moving boxes. Moreover, the government will pay for the shipment of professional books to your next duty station. And finally, if you do not have or cannot make time to read at least fifteen minutes a day, you simply are not trying. A good professional library is one of the pillars of your professional growth. Most of the books cited are reasonably priced, easy to order, and, best of all, well written with you in mind.

These twenty-some books will well serve you throughout your naval career. The United States Naval Institute (of course, you are already a member) is a ready source for most of them. The Institute is the principal publisher of naval professional books worldwide.

About Your Duties

Mack, William P., Harry A. Seymour Jr., and Lesa A. McComas. *The Naval Officer's Guide,* 11th ed. Annapolis, Md.: Naval Institute Press. 1998.
Stavridis, James, and William P. Mack. *Command at Sea,* 5th ed. Annapolis, Md.: Naval Institute Press. 1998.

Stavridis, James. *The Division Officer's Guide,* 10th edition. Annapolis, Md.: Naval Institute Press. 1995.

Stavridis, James. *The Watch Officer's Guide,* 14th ed. Annapolis, Md.: Naval Institute Press. 1999.

Winters, David D. *The Boat Officer's Handbook,* 2nd ed. Annapolis, Md.: Naval Institute Press. 1991.

About Your Professional Skills

Barber, James A. *Naval Shiphander's Guide.* Annapolis, Md.: Naval Institute Press. 2005.

Dodge, David O., and S. E. Kyriss. *Seamanship: Fundamentals for the Deck Officer,* 2nd ed. Annapolis, Md.: Naval Institute Press. 1981.

Llana, Christopher B. and George P. Wisneskey. *Handbook of Nautical Rules of the Road: A Convenient Take-Along Guide for Sail and Power Boaters.* Annapolis, Md.: Naval Institute Press. 1991.

Montor, Karel. *Naval Leadership: Voices of Experience,* 2nd ed. Annapolis, Md.: Naval Institute Press. 1998.

Noel, John V., Jr. *Knight's Modern Seamanship,* 18th ed. New York: John Wiley & Sons. 1989.

Shenk, Robert. *Guide to Naval Writing,* 2nd ed. Annapolis, Md.: Naval Institute Press. 1997.

Strunk, William, Jr., and E. B. White. *The Elements of Style,* 4th ed. New York: Allyn and Bacon, 2000.

About the Service

Benitez, Rafael. *Anchors: Ethical and Practical Maxims.* Annapolis, Md.: Annapolis Publishing Company. 1996.

Burgess, Richard R. *The Naval Aviation Guide,* 5th ed. Annapolis, Md.: Naval Institute Press. 1996.

Calvert, James. *The Naval Profession,* rev. ed. New York: McGraw-Hill. 1965.

Cutler, Thomas J. *The Bluejacket's Manual,* Centennial ed. Annapolis, Md.: Naval Institute Press. 2002.

Filbert, Brent G. and Alan G. Kaufman. *Naval Law: Justice and Procedures in the Sea Services,* 3rd ed. Annapolis, Md.: Naval Institute Press. 1998.

Mack, William P. and Royal W. Connell. *Naval Ceremonies, Customs, and Traditions,* 6th ed. Annapolis, Md.: Naval Institute Press. 2004.

Noel, John V., Jr. and Edward L. Beach. *Naval Terms Dictionary,* 5th ed. Annapolis, Md.: Naval Institute Press. 1988.

Schwartz, Oretha. *Service Etiquette,* 4th ed. Annapolis, Md.: Naval Institute Press. 1988.

Stavridis, Laura Hall. *The Navy Spouse's Guide,* 2nd ed. Annapolis, Md.: Naval Institute Press. 2002.

Notes

Chapter 3. What Are They Saying about You?

1. John Masters, *Bugles and a Tiger: A Personal Adventure* (New York: Viking, 1956), 121. This book is an excellent distillation of experience gained the hard way in adjusting to service life as a junior officer.

Chapter 4. Mentors and Cliques

1. This change is an example of the danger of relying on a single snapshot of service practices. Past attempts to institutionalize officer mentoring, as recently as the mid-1990s, have failed. If some institutionalization occurs, as seems likely, it could be viewed either as a significant change or as an extension of counseling required by current fitness report preparation directives.

2. See Carl Graham, "Take the Roll of the Dice out of the Selection Process," *Proceedings* vol. 129, no. 12 (December 2003): 59. This article is a balanced critique of the Navy's screening and promotion systems by an officer who failed to screen for command. It suggests, however, that mentors and influence are critical to screening and promotion. I disagree; performance is the critical element. Mentors and influence may help performance on the margin but are not the central element of career success. One of the purposes of the book before the reader is to respond to Graham's suggestion that the Navy needs to "open the drapes a little and minimize [the perception of] the luck, timing, and who-you-know aspect of the selection process."

Chapter 5. The Wardroom and Ready Room Menagerie

1. Communication from Vice Adm. Robert F. Dunn, USN (Ret.)

2. John Masters asserts that the motto of the professional fighting man is "Never explain, never complain." Masters, *Bugles and a Tiger,* 115.

Chapter 6. Spring Training

1. As quoted in Robert D. Heinl, *Dictionary of Military and Naval Quotations* (Annapolis, Md.: Naval Institute Press, 1966), 88.

Chapter 7. Do You Shine in the Career Marketplace?

1. C. S. Forester, *Hornblower and the Hotspur* (Boston: Little, Brown, 1962), 13.

Chapter 8. Been to School Lately?

1. Contrast Navy career patterns and educational practices with the Air Force and Army, where a soldier-scholar or airman-scholar can still prosper in fast-track billets. If you need proof of the Navy view, ask any of the assignment officers in the Naval Personnel Command how difficult a time they have in filling quotas for technical postgraduate curricula (two years or longer) with top-performing officers.

Chapter 9. Sea/Shore Rotation and Homesteading

1. A common characteristic of flag officer career summaries is that most of these officers had a succession of short tours because their talents were in demand—not necessarily because they were billet hopping to touch all bases. As in civilian life, scarce, expensive, and capable resources are often redeployed frequently to maximize system output. You should not seek a succession of short assignments, but if they should come your way, it may be an indication of your visibility and marketability in the personnel assignment system.

2. A little-recognized fact is that most newly minted flag officers have gone to sea for the last time. Only those capable enough to get command of a group afloat or a numbered fleet go back to sea. Those who remain ashore will likely spend the rest of their service in Washington or other shore headquarters.

3. Private communication to the author.

4. In the Navy I grew up in, the same thing could be said about being assigned to public quarters (i.e., Navy housing). If you were a comer, public quarters were not in your future (except for some command billets) until you made flag. And most flag officers in Washington did not (and do not) reside in public quarters. This rankled some fast-track officers while in their sea command in San Diego and Norfolk. They were denied quarters because of rank, billet, expected tour lengths, waiting lists, and so on. Most of the available public quarters were occupied by long-tour staffers (including staff corps and restricted line) rather than seagoing officers. My Naval Academy classmate Vice Adm. Joe Metcalf reminds me, "The staff always looks out for itself!"

5. Private communication to the author.

Chapter 10. Command and Staff Assignments

1. James Calvert, *The Naval Profession* (New York: McGraw-Hill, 1965), 165–66.

Chapter 11. Washington Duty

1. In recent years, with the reorganization and consolidation of the functions of the main fleet commanders, some important force sizing, program, and readiness functions have been pushed out of Washington to the various fleet, joint, and combined commands in Norfolk and San Diego. For every generality there is an exception, and such is the case here.

Chapter 12. Career Tracks for the Unrestricted Line

1. The timing of the executive officer tour varies by warfare community. In aviation, XOs fleet up to become COs except for aircraft carriers and some naval air stations.

2. The aviators' path for major command at sea has three alternative tracks: (1) deputy air wing commander to air wing commander, (2) command of a deep draft ship (e.g., oiler) to command of an aircraft carrier, and (3) executive officer of a major amphibious ship (LHA, LHD) to commanding officer of that ship. A few aviators go on from their deep draft ships to command an amphibious or service squadron. The fleeting-up concept is typical of aviation command at the squadron and air wing levels.

3. Communication from a former detailer.

4. The term "Washington area headquarters" refers to all billets in the Pentagon, the various systems commands including those at the nearby Naval Air Test Center at Patuxent River, Maryland; the Navy Personnel Command at Millington, Tennessee; and smaller shore facilities and labs in the national capital area.

5. From time to time, three- and four-star officers are polled informally and discretely as to the best and brightest of the one- and two-star officers, and the results are available to be used in the process of picking the next three-star candidates.

6. There have been a few cases of excellent and specially qualified officers getting three back-to-back three-star tours. Each is a special case that can be explained on the basis that an expected four-star slot did not open up as expected.

Chapter 13. Promotion to Flag Rank

1. The phenomenon of rising to one's level of incompetence is sometimes called the "Peter Principle" after the works of C. Northcote Parkinson. There is a simple but important point in this jibe. In the Navy some officers are very adept ship or squadron skippers where they can be hands on. If there is a problem in their command they can go right to the source and take corrective action. Flag officers are largely denied this luxury. They must more often deal through others, some of whom are geographically removed from headquarters. They deal through layers of subordinates and are sometimes late in receiving vital information. In short, they must work through remote control to correct or anticipate problems. One of the most important tasks of flag officers in command is to establish systems and procedures that keep them informed and facilitate timely and effective actions. The changes in this imperative from ship to battle group to fleet are each of a different order of magnitude, and some officers find it difficult to adjust to the new circumstances of command. Too often they rely on what worked for them in their last job, rather than on what their new circumstances require.

2. Recent changes in the management of flag numbers permit a limited number of such officers to continue on active service beyond the thirty-five-year point.

Chapter 14. Awards and Decorations

1. Compare with the Army dress tunic, which displays a snapshot of the officer's career with its many stripes, badges, unit affiliations, decorations, and achievement awards.

2. Previous to the establishment of joint medals that currently parallel the services' own systems, a joint command wishing to commend an officer initiated a recommendation for an award from the officer's own service. But there were problems in such a simple solution: each service handled such joint recommendations differently, and two officers from different services in the same office doing the same job found that their parent services had acted differently on the joint commander's award recommendations.

Chapter 15. Pass the (Social) Polish, Please

1. One should not be afraid of "brilliant flashes of silence," a phrase attributed to Sydney Smith and quoted in Reece Gronow's *The Reminiscences and*

Recollections of Captain Gronow, 1810–1860 (New York: Viking Press, 1964), 236.

Chapter 16. The Navy Spouse

1. Calvert, *The Naval Profession,* 90.
2. Laura Hall Staviridis, the daughter and wife of naval officers, has written a very useful little handbook that I recommend to all Navy spouses and spouses-to-be: *Navy Spouse's Guide* (Annapolis, Md.: Naval Institute Press, 2002).

Chapter 17. Assignment and Placement Officers

1. Communication of a former detailer with the author.
2. A joint billet is one in which the officer assigned works with representatives of the other service (e.g., Joint Staff). A combined billet is one in which the assigned officer works with the representatives of other nations (e.g., NATO).
3. There are exceptions. An officer who has not served in a joint and combined billet and who has been selected for flag rank serves his first flag assignment in a joint flag billet.
4. Graham, "Take the Roll of the Dice." Graham is speaking specifically to the screening and promotion systems, but similar criticism is leveled at the assignment system that is upstream of screening and promotions.

Chapter 18. The Fitness Report System

1. The current directive (as this was written) is BUPERSINST 1610.10, "Navy Performance Evaluation and Counseling System" (August 2, 1995), as updated by various administrative messages intended to reduce the fitness report rejection rate and further fine-tune the directive. The meat of this directive resides in the *Navy Performance Evaluation and Counseling Manual.*
2. We will not discuss such specialized reports as concurrent and operations commander reports. The reader is referred to BUPERSINST 1610.10, Annexes E and F.
3. For documented facts, consider the following examples: "His department won the force engineering E for the period he served as engineering officer." "He was the top graduate in his fighter weapons school class." "She was the honor graduate at nuclear power school." "He was the only officer of his rank in the air wing (or squadron) to be selected to represent the command in a select study group established by the type commander to consider ways to improve

unit readiness." "The reenlistment rate in her department was the highest for similar departments in the entire force."

Chapter 19. Screening and Promotion Boards

1. In recent years much of record collecting and summarizing processes have become partially or fully automated. One board recorder told the author that "now that our time-tested but highly impractical microfiche is being replaced by an on-line record review, an officer has no excuse for not knowing what is in his or her record. An officer's entire career—ten, fifteen, twenty, or twenty-five years of toil and sacrifice—is distilled down to three or four sheets of fitness report and background data for board members to consider. Typographical errors, blanks, and incorrect entries matter."

2. For example, see SECNAVINST 1401.3 of December 1, 1989, "Selection Board Membership." Board representation for unrestricted line officers (URL) is specified to be proportionate to the breakout of URL officers by warfare community.

3. But in most cases passed-over lieutenant commanders may remain on duty until the twenty-year point, and passed-over commanders may remain for twenty-six years.

4. One screening board recorder says that unofficial board feedback should be taken with a grain of salt, and he suggests that officers who failed to screen should not base their next career move on what they were told by someone who was present or who claims to have spoken with someone who was.

5. The delays in the case of the more-senior boards are caused by the extensive security vetting required and by the fact that in some cases the board results must be reviewed by the Joint Staff for the chairman and various officials in the Office of the Secretary of Defense before being approved and the list sent to the White House.

Chapter 20. Advice for Midshipmen

1. Even if you are in business for yourself in civilian life, you will complain about federal and state regulations that govern the conduct of your business. Your scope of action may be large but is nevertheless framed by others—the market, the competition, or the "feds."

2. Many fast-track patrol aviators and flight officers, during their second sea tour or sometimes in their third sea tour, are ordered to what is called a

"disassociated tour." This tour, typically in a carrier, may involve service as assistant navigator or in any of a number of air or operations department billets. Most patrol (VP)-trained flag officers of my acquaintance followed this route.

Chapter 21. Advice for Those Who Have Missed a Hurdle

1. This was in 1948, after the landmark Officer Personnel Act of 1947 had been enacted into law. That law established, among other things, the benchmarks of a naval career in terms of years of service and promotion percentages to each grade. Though since superceded, that law provides the framework for the current officer personnel management system.

2. But at least one flag officer does not agree with this advice. He believes there is insufficient time to change duty stations and get a meaningful fitness report before the next board convenes. His point has merit. But a board can be impressed by an officer who just missed but who goes to a tough job for another time at bat.

3. Hamilton Basso, *The View from Pompey's Head* (New York: Doubleday, 1954), 204.

4. Rafael C. Benitez, *Anchors: Ethical and Practical Maxims* (Annapolis, Md.: Annapolis Publishing, 1996), 24. Any officer would benefit from reading this little handbook and putting its advice into practice.

5. Ibid., 16.

6. I once had a shipmate whose motto was "Keep one guy between you and the problem." His career had an unhappy ending.

Appendix A: Dilemmas and Paradoxes in a Naval Career

1. For those with little or no familiarity with the service, I should point out that this point underpins the prevalent practice at Navy ceremonies of expressing gratitude to Navy spouses and families for the loyal support and the sacrifices they have routinely made.

2. The place of nuclear power training in the Navy's education scheme is an ambiguous one. Some would maintain that the rigor, focus, and content of nuclear power training are such that it is in effect a postgraduate course of instruction. To qualify you must pass a rigorous selection process and demonstrate solid engineering credentials. Nuclear power training not only imparts significant scientific and practical knowledge but also stamps a distinct

mind-set on its graduates, a mind-set that prizes discipline, intellectual integrity, and analytic rigor—all with a focus on the practical application of those mental tools. For reasons best known to those who direct the nuclear power training pipeline, there has been little support in that community for awarding postgraduate degrees to the program's graduates. One influential officer in that program remarked to the author, "We are in the training business, not the credentialing business." This answer suggests that credentialing nuclear power training graduates might lead to a lowered retention rate of these valuable resources.

Appendix B: All Detailing Is Local

1. An extract from Clay Harris's article, "Science Does Not Trump Art," *Proceedings* vol. 129, no. 7 (July 2003): 62.

Index

About the Author

Rear Adm. James A. Winnefeld graduated from the Naval Academy in 1951. He has served in destroyers, aircraft carriers and their embarked squadrons, and amphibious ships. After four commands at sea, both in aviation and surface warfare units, he served as commandant of midshipmen. His early knowledge of the Navy's performance rating, promotion, and assignment systems was gained in three tours in the Bureau of Naval Personnel and in seeing those systems work (or not) from the deck plates. He served on a wide variety of personnel selection boards.

After his retirement from the Navy, Rear Admiral Winnefeld was a program director for RAND, a policy analysis think tank for the government. While at RAND he conducted strategy and personnel management studies for the services, the combatant commands, the Department of State, the Director of Central Intelligence, and the White House. Over the years since his retirement, he has maintained close ties with many former and current midshipmen. Their aspirations and questions about a naval career prompted the writing of this book.

Rear Admiral Winnefeld is the son, nephew, brother, and father of Navy men who served afloat in peace and war. He has a deep affection and respect for the Navy and its men and women.